THE ELEVENTH HOUR

The Eleventh Hour
EXPLOSION OF A CHURCH

by FRANÇOIS HOUTART

edited by Mary Anne Chouteau
with an Introduction by HARVEY COX

SHEED AND WARD: *New York*

© *Sheed & Ward, Inc., 1968*

Library of Congress Catalog Card Number 68–13856

Nihil Obstat:
> *Brendan W. Lawlor*
> *Censor Librorum*

Imprimatur:
> *† Robert F. Joyce*
> *Bishop of Burlington*
> *January 12, 1968*

Manufactured in the United States of America

EDITOR'S NOTE

Material for this book was edited from lectures by Canon
Houtart given during a Pastoral Institute for Priests at
Conception Abbey, Missouri, in July and August of 1966
and completed from notes in the course on the Sociology
of Pastoral Work given by the author at Louvain University, Belgium, in 1966–67.

CONTENTS

7

INTRODUCTION

It was the best of times. It was the worst of times. It was a time of hope and a time of frustration. It was a time when some people thought the Church was changing too fast and others thought it was not changing fast enough. In short it was the time *after* the Vatican Council but *before* its ideas had really done much to change the structures of the Church. Indeed by the beginning of 1968 many hearts which had beaten high during the exciting days of the Vatican Council had slowed to a normal pulse. The euphoria had subsided. People began to grumble about the loss of momentum and the return to rigidity. Bishops who had voted with the future in Rome many times drifted into the past when they returned to their own dioceses. Feelings of elation and expectation on the part of many lay people cooled into discouragement and bickering. Despite the grand promise of the Council, the Roman Catholic Church had not achieved an instant aggiornamento. Disquieted individuals began to mutter that the whole thing was an illusion. But was it?

Of course it was not. True, an "underground Church" emerged which at some points seemed to have lost confidence in the mutability of Church structures. Also there seemed to be a falling off of the numbers of young men entering seminaries. There were other signs of dissatisfaction. Properly understood, however, the "underground Church" is a sign of hope. It shows that many Catholics are taking their responsibility to experiment and innovate with real seriousness. Also the dissatisfaction and unrest among seminarians, clergy and nuns is encouraging. It reveals not only a readiness but a real eagerness to find new ways of bridging the artificial gap between the sacred and the secular worlds. All in all, it seems undeniable that something extremely important is happening in the Catholic Church, although it often seems more impressive to non-Catholics than to Catholics.

The trouble with most of the changes so far, however, is that they often take the form of a new spirit and a fresh vitality rather than of modifications in structure. It is clear by now, however, that if the earliest hopes engendered by the Council are to be fulfilled, the impulse to reform must move out from the spirit and transform the body. If change and renewal are not institutionalized they will quickly evaporate, leaving only a residue of shattered hopes and bitterness.

The appearance of François Houtart's book on the reform of the institutional Church provides an excellent occasion for Catholics and all Christians to think once again about what they really had expected from the Council. More important, it forces all of us to ask ourselves what must be done to implement its declarations. Without any doubt some of the hopes it quickened were too sanguine. *How* can an institution as old, as immense and as cumbersome as the Roman Catholic Church change? That is the hard question which people have begun to ask more recently. Advocates of aggiornamento had learned that even when a lot of people want something, actually making it happen requires both a knowledge of how change comes about in institutions and a strategy for inducing it.

In this book Houtart looks at the Church through the hard unsentimental eyes of a sociologist. No romantic radical, neither is he an anti-institutional Arcadian. He examines the values of collegiality, freedom and personal responsibility as they have been enunciated by the Council and then shows how these values, not without severe strain, can assume institutional form in the Church. With this book, change in the Church moves from rhetoric to reform, from talk to tactics, from slogans to strategies. For those who have given up on any possibility of changing the Church the book will seem like a futile gesture. For those who are quite content to keep things as they are it will appear to be a threat. But for those who wish to see the spirit of the Council implemented in the Church, are looking for concrete means to make this actually happen, this book is a godsend.

Perhaps the single most important insight Houtart offers is that tension in an organization is not a curse to be avoided but a sign of health. Tension indicates that the organization, in this case the Church, is undergoing the pain and distress which are the necessary byproducts of genuine change. An institution in which there is no tension is a dead or dying one. An institution which is able not only to funnel and accommodate tension but even to generate it is a live one. For Houtart, who welcomes the tension we all notice in the Church today, the question therefore is not just how to manage it but how to make sure it continues to appear.

Part of his answer is to be found in his advocacy of structures of authentic participation. When people really take part in making the decisions in any organization rather than living as second-class citizens, the questions of both how tension is handled and how it is managed are that much closer to solution. Where offices of authority are viewed as a means of facilitating communication and corporate thinking, and not as a bludgeon by which some people tell others what to do, the health of any organization is increased. Houtart spells out how he thinks this can happen.

From what I have said so far it should be clear that this book will not be of interest only to Catholics. Members of any and all Churches must face similar problems as the challenge to change pursues us all. Houtart's analysis, with few exceptions, applies to all religious institutions. Indeed for many Protestants it may seem as though it was written expressly for them. Do Catholics labor under fossilized structures? For many non-Catholics the fossilization is even worse, but it is hidden under a cloud of Protestant rhetoric about the "ministry of the laity" and the "autonomy of the congregation." Do many Catholics feel themselves stifled by diocesan structures? How many Protestant laymen really feel they have much to say about what happens in their denominational headquarters? At least Catholics have the impulse of the Council going for them. Many Protestants labor under the facile delusion that Protestantism doesn't need an aggiornamento. But it does, and the non-Catholic reader of this book is bound to be struck by both the similarity of the problems and the viability of Houtart's answers.

We are safe in saying about the renewal of the Churches what Mark Twain said about the weather: Everyone talks about it, but no one does anything about it. So far this has too often been the case. However, for those who are willing to take the step from palaver to pioneering this book is a good place to begin.

HARVEY COX

Dia de Reyes (Jan. 6)
San Juan, Puerto Rico

PREFACE

Almost all revolutions are provoked by a cultural lag between new values and old institutions. The Catholic Church, in this period of transition from the pre-conciliar to the post-conciliar Church, is being described by many analysts as existing in a "pre-revolutionary" situation.

The new values of participation, collegiality, freedom, and personal responsibility set forth in the documents of Vatican II are meeting with resistance from structures within the Church which have become rigid with age and tradition, and many are questioning whether these new values can become a part of the institutional Church in time to avoid a crisis of open revolution or of quiet defection.

Adaptation is made more difficult within the institutional Church because of the rapid social change which is affecting all of secular society and, since "the world" is the field of Christian activity, the Church as well.

15

So the Church is living through a period of profound change both without and within, science and technology being the main agents of change in secular society and the Second Vatican Council the expression of change within the Church.

It is a fact of human experience that every institution tends to be conservative. Its role is to "institutionalize" values, and this means to give them some continuity and stability. The same thing is true for the Church because she is not something which exists outside mankind. This is really one of the great mysteries of the Church: that Christ founded his Church within mankind, under the guidance of the Holy Spirit but, as an institution, subject to the normal laws of human growth and development. It is not because we are preaching the Gospel, for example, that our voices may be heard miles away, but because we are using microphones or the communications satellite. Even for the evangelization of the world God respects the laws of nature.

This is true, also, of the social laws. We should not think that because of its divine origin the Church as an institution for our salvation will operate under some special system, different from that of all other institutions or exempt from their problems. It should not be an occasion of scandal for us if we find tensions and difficulties of adaptation in the Church. We must be very realistic about this. In the past we have had such an "angelic" image of the Church in many ways that we have gone to some lengths to suppress knowledge of tensions and difficulties, to avoid giving scandal. The Second Vatican Council has given us a new vision of the Church, and it is with this approach in mind that we shall examine it as institution and the changes brought by the Council.

An institution owes its existence to the aims or purposes for which it was established, and can be judged in accordance with its success or failure in furthering those aims. The main aspect of an institution is not its organization, but the values lived and expressed in it. This is also true for the Church, although she differs from other institutions in this respect: while their aims may change or be changed or simply be abandoned, the ultimate aims of the Church are always the same. Her understanding of these aims, however, is constantly growing and developing under the guidance of the Holy Spirit.

When we study the Church as institution then, even though a sociological approach is used, we must at all times keep a theological perspective. The Church is a living body whose mission is to show forth Christ, the light of the world, to all peoples until the will of the Father—the salvation of all men in Christ—is accomplished. But this is always a mission to living men; it is a mission of the present and for the future. In order to accomplish this mission, therefore, the Church must always be ready to change those aspects of her institutional presence and teaching in the world which do not really witness to her unchanging mission but witness only to a culture of the past. It is only if the Church is able to read the "signs of the times"—God's continuing presence in the unfolding universe he has created—that she will be able to give witness in a changing world to what is of lasting value for man.

This was the main emphasis of *The Challenge to Change*. I tried, in that book, to show in particular two things—that the Church had nothing to fear from change and that our scientific and technical civilization has brought the world to a stage of incessant change which will be permanent: the "challenge" was for the Church to meet this reality with courage and audacity. The Council was then just beginning. The Constitution on the Church in the Modern World had not yet come into being, and the work of preparation was painful, for it had first to be established that change was not only normal but necessary for the Church if she were to fulfill her mission in the world.

Now the Council is over, and we are living in a new period. Tensions and insecurities abound. Some people attribute all these difficulties to the Council and look back on the period before it as one of unbroken tranquillity. Others think that the Council has spoken the last word on change in the Church. It is more realistic to say that the Council initiated in the Church a movement which cannot be stopped. But the Council is over, and despite its extraordinary accomplishments it will very soon seem to bear the marks of its time. However, it remains true that it took a major step in the history of the Church, one with more profound implications than many have yet realized. The consequences, therefore, are far-reaching and sometimes unexpected.

Taking a sociological approach, I will try to show how the Church as an institution has been transformed by the Council. Such an approach does not pretend to give an answer to all the problems faced by the Church today, nor does it propose many startling innovations. But it may provide a better understanding of these problems by placing them in perspective. We are so accustomed to thinking of the Church as a supernatural reality that we are not prepared for the very human confusion which results when, as an institution composed of men which she also is, she undertakes an *aggiornamento.*

For methodological reasons the situation of the Church before Vatican II and after Vatican II will have to be expressed in "types." This results in reducing the reality to some of its major components and in simplifying the situation to some degree. There is, of course, no "pre-conciliar" or "post-conciliar" Church with respect to many of the questions we will discuss, but a kind of *continuum.* Nevertheless the Second Vatican Council has marked an epoch, and it is not illegitimate to take it as a point of departure.

THE ELEVENTH HOUR

1 THE CHURCH AND HER AIMS: NEW PERSPECTIVES

There are many ways to study an institution. We are not, for example, going to make an empirical study to see how the Church would be described by an observation of her actions and of how she looks in the world, although this is one way, and a very instructive one. We shall start with the definition the Church gave of herself and with the reformulation of aims which is implicit in the Council documents in order to make a few observations about their consequences for the Church as an institution. It should be understood that in any institution decisions regarding its definition and its aims are of central importance because modification in such areas will bring about a whole series of transformations, sometimes unexpected but quite normal. These may be called—to use the term of American sociologist Philip Selznick—"critical decisions," because they affect the whole life and organization of an institution.

23

THE REDEFINITION OF THE CHURCH

First of all, and most important, the Council redefined the Church, giving pre-eminence to the definition of the Church as the *People of God*. When we look at the facts of recent history, we see that this definition represents a profound change in our conception of the Church. Not that it is a new definition—it is biblical—but it holds very new implications for the organization of the Church as we now know it.

We have had, in the past, a vision of the Church as juridical and monarchical, a pyramid with the Pope at the top, the bishops below him, the priests still lower, and the laity at the base. The Constitution on the Church has effaced this image by redefining the Church in scriptural terms. God called together all who believe in Jesus Christ into one people; this is the main reality and this is the Church, the People of God. All the rest is, in a certain sense, accidental—not in the sense that Christ did not establish a hierarchical Church but in the sense that the pyramidal structure was patterned very much according to the historical conditions in which the Church developed. By defining the function of the hierarchy in scriptural terms the Council document has placed the accent on service, not dominion. The hierarchy is *for* the people.

Every institution needs an authority, but the way an authority is exercised depends on the kinds of values the group expresses. The role of authority is to keep cohesion in a group. Before the Council, owing to the survival into modern times of a medieval structure in the Church, the authority had *the* central place in the Church. In *Lumen Gentium,* the Constitution on the Church, it is clearly defined in *functional* terms as a ministry to the group. This does not mean a denial of the authority of the bishops as pastors who keep the flock together, but the authority is no longer part of a "sacralized" juridical power structure. Since the role of the laity in the apostolate is seen as coming, not as a mandate from the hierarchy but from their baptism, the accent has been placed on the freedom which believers must enjoy, for the Holy Spirit breathes where he will.

Now that the accent has been placed on the actual participation of all the members of the people of God in the whole life of the institution, with the hierarchy seen as ministering to the people of God, we simply cannot conceive that all these people will no longer have anything to say about the organization of the Church or its concrete actions. Most probably empirical data would still indicate the contrary: that the Church is still a very businesslike, authoritarian structure where the people have not much to say about the institutional life and very little, if anything, to say about their understanding of the mission of the Church in the world. This would be an accurate picture in most instances, because it will take time for the new orientation given by the Council to be realized in the Church, and it is possible for it to be blocked or delayed by resistance.

However, the whole accomplishment of the plan of God as set forth in Genesis and developed throughout the rest of revelation is a process of increasing rational control by man of himself and the world and a convergence of all creation towards the fullness of all created things in Christ through the action of the Holy Spirit. Every step forward in the field of rationality brings with it increased responsibility, makes man more a man than he was before and more like God, in whose image he was created, with a creative intelligence which is the mark of his spiritual nature. And it is this vision of creation and redemption which has been seen by the Council and written into its documents. There is a recognition of the development of doctrine, which is a growth in our understanding of the gospel message, and an awareness that God is the Lord of history. The growing consciousness of the dignity of the human person and his right to responsible action in all areas of his life which we see in mankind today comes from God and is to be respected by the Church: this understanding was fundamental to the Church's self-reflection during the Second Vatican Council, as the best ways were sought to be true to her mission in the world today.

The emphasis on *participation*, then, is of prime importance, and it influenced and oriented many of the Council's decisions. It is perhaps true that not all the bishops voting for the Constitution on the Church fully realized the explosive matter which it contained, but the Holy Spirit was present at the Council too!

So it is in view of this emphasis on participation that we shall be able to interpret fully all the documents of the Council in their implementation in the post-conciliar Church, even those voted on before the Constitution on the Church. The Constitution on the Liturgy really prepared the way for the Constitution on the Church because it restored the active role of the entire people of God in worship and opened the way for a more complete understanding of both the external and internal aims of the Church.

In other words the fact that the Church has been defined in the second chapter of *Lumen Gentium* as the People of God has a fundamental importance for the whole ecclesiastical institution. An important value receives a privileged place: the fact that the members of the Church are seen as constituting the ecclesiastical reality rather than as "subjects" of the ecclesiastical organization.

The definition of the Church in terms of people rather than in terms of organization not only marks a change in relationship between the laity and the hierarchy in the Catholic Church, it also brings about a profound reorientation in the relations between the Roman Catholic Church and the other Christian Churches.

The change in our relations with other Christians has been a gradual process based on the preparation of pre-

vious reflection and experience. In creating a new awareness of the Church's mission of reconciliation, the influence of Pope John XXIII was especially important. Not
only his own open personality but his setting up of a permanent secretariat for promoting Christian Unity, even
before the Council, paved the way for a new type of relationship. With the Council the Catholic Church passed
officially from an attitude of hostility to one of peaceful
coexistence, and finally to one of cooperation with other
Christians. In the Council documents this cooperation has
been extended to three areas: to certain studies in theology, to prayer in common under certain regulations,
and to common concern and collaboration on social questions and problems.

But more than a change in attitude toward other
Christians resulted from the Council. There was a subtle
but definite change in the way the Church is described in
the passage of the Constitution on the Church referring to
the Church of Jesus Christ which "subsists" in the Catholic Church. This word is repeated again in the document
on Religious Freedom. The vision which it evokes of the
other Christian Churches is quite different from what we
have known in the past: "This Church, constituted and
organized in the world as a society, subsists in the Catholic Church, which is governed by the successor of Peter
and by the bishops in union with that successor, although
many elements of sanctification and truth can be found
outside her visible structure. These elements, however, as

gifts properly belonging to the Church of Christ, possess an inner dynamism toward Catholic unity."[1] The consequences of this acknowledgment of the "ecclesial elements" in other Christian Churches are very important for the future of Christian unity.

The Church has also been defined as a sacrament, or a "sign"—a definition now commonly held in Christianity by both Protestants and Catholics. As a sign "of close union with God and of the unity of the whole of mankind," as Vatican II describes her, the Church is to be both the *manifestation* of a reality which is only indirectly apprehended and the *announcement* of something which will happen in the future.

As a sign of the union of God with all mankind, which gives a new dimension to the meaning of the world and to human life, the Church has a responsibility, then, not only to all Christians but to all men.

If the Church is to be a manifestation of the union of God with the whole of mankind, such a manifestation of the divine will be a manifestation of another *dimension* of the world and of human life, and not a ritualistic alienation, or just a code of morality, or a social or psychological function of society. Faith will not function as a substitute for human responsibility or human potentiality, but to give a meaning to man's actions in the world and a more acute sense of his full human responsibility.

[1] *The Documents of Vatican II*, ed. Walter M. Abbot, S.J. (New York: Guild Press, America Press, Association Press, 1966), p. 23.

In this sense it implies a full acceptance of secularization, of what Harvey Cox calls the "disenchantment of
nature" and the Constitution on the Church in the Modern
World calls a respect for the "autonomy of the temporal
order." God is not at work in the world in the sense of
setting aside its proper laws; his presence in the world is
mediated through the intelligence and liberty of men for
the restoration of all things in Christ. God is present in
all human efforts to perfect the temporal order and bring
it to fulfillment.

The redefinition of the Church as the People of God,
subsisting in the Catholic Church, the sign of close union
with God and of the unity of the whole of mankind, will
affect, first of all, the perception and understanding of all
the aims of the Church.

THE REDEFINITION OF HER AIMS

The simplest definition of the Church is a grouping of the
people having faith in Jesus Christ. But even in this simple
definition it is possible to discover two kinds of aims,
which are divisible for the sake of discussion but actually
cannot be separated: *external aims* and *internal aims*.
This may seem to be complicating a simple definition, but
if having faith in Christ (internal aim) means also accepting his mandate to go forth and teach all nations,
this implies a reference to the world (external aim).

The external aims of the Church in reference to the world are threefold:

> *to announce salvation in Jesus Christ,*
>
> *to invite all men having faith in Christ to an assembly of the people of God, i.e., to a church,* and *to act in the world in terms of the Gospel.*

In reference to herself, the Church has two main internal aims:

> *the internalization of values and norms in each individual member* and *the cohesion of the group.*

It is extremely important when studying the whole problem of the organization of the Church that we be aware of these aims, because all our ways of action have to correspond to them. It is necessary to remember, too, that no institution exists for its own sake, not even the Church, but that each institution is a mixture of values (aims) and organization, and has certain internal requisites in order to function.

External Aims: Christ in the World

As a result of the Council, there has been a transformation of understanding in terms of the external aims of the Church: to announce the Gospel to all men; to invite believers in Christ to an assembly, and to act in the world.

This transformation of understanding did not come about all at once, of course, and in fact there is still a long way to go. But we see that the Council did make some very fundamental changes of orientation in terms of our previous understanding of the external mission of the Church to the world.

After the Middle Ages the missionary movement in the Church almost came to a halt because the Church was so well organized in society that the feeling and the theory prevailed that a person who was not a Christian was himself responsible for that fact. It was his fault and not the fault of the Church. This attitude was also prevalent at the end of the fifteenth century during the evangelization of Latin America by the Spaniards and the Portuguese.

During the next two centuries the missionary movement almost stopped, only to be revived during the European colonial period, when colonization was used as a new channel for opening up the rest of the world to the Church. By this time the Church was very European in her institutional manifestation and had been so for some centuries. Little effort was made to understand the cultural differences of the countries to which the faith was brought. Missionaries learned to speak the language of the people and made a few very minor symbolic adaptations.

The concept of the mission as understood at this time was to bring *more* people into the Church. It was really a

quantitative approach and explains to some degree, though it cannot excuse, some of the methods of proselytizing used during several centuries of the Church's history.

So quantitative had our approach become that the only statistics kept by the Church were in terms of the numbers of converts. In addition to a quantitative approach, the Church's missionary work became closely associated with the transmission of Western culture. It was built around the prestige of the white man and his technical superiority, especially in Africa and Asia, and this attitude greatly influenced the whole formation and training of missionaries.

With the exception of the Jesuits in China and in India in the fifteenth century, it is only since about 1925, after World War I, that the idea of adaptation to the culture of the people was seriously considered, although at the very earliest times of the Church, St. Paul had argued much the same problem with St. Peter in regard to Gentile converts. One could have hoped that the principle might have been similarly applied throughout the centuries after this first period in the Church, but unfortunately it was not. It has been only recently that new conscious effort is being made to understand cultures very different from our own so that the faith can be really transmitted to these cultures.

The subconscious reaction of peoples of the non-Western cultures evangelized with a "quantitative" approach

has sometimes resulted in such an incomplete assimilation of the faith that many syncretisms exist. And often, where the evangelization has been more complete, the accompanying Westernization has succeeded in creating small "ghettoes" within the country, so that the Church cannot really be said to be present in these cultures. We have seen the results of this very recently in Africa, and also in Ceylon and India; some of these countries began to close their doors to missionaries, and part of the reason was that missionaries have appeared as representative of foreign powers and have remained aliens.

The fact that the percentage of Catholics in the world has remained the same (19%) since the First Vatican Council and will probably drop to about 15% by the year 2000 because of the population explosion in non-Christian countries indicates that a quantitative approach is neither adequate nor appropriate.

One effect of the Council on the external aims of the Church has been an emphasis placed on a *qualitative* rather than a quantitative approach to missiology. It is not just a matter of individual conversions, but a collective aim, that of bringing the people of the whole world, with all their varying cultures, into the People of God, to make them active participants in the life of the Church and of the world. So this must be seen to be a very long-range objective, one requiring a collective witness on the part of the Church, and one which may never culminate in a visible, world-wide People of God on this earth. But

the witness of the Church must take place within *all* cultures because "the People of God" is certainly not synonymous with "Western culture."

The recognition of the values of non-Christian religions and of the fact that Christ is at work in these cultures, made by the Decree on Non-Christian Religions and the chapter on culture of *Gaudium et Spes,* furnish the base for a very new approach to the first two external aims of the Church: to announce the salvation in Jesus Christ and to invite the believers to an assembly: the Church. For a long time the destruction in the converts of the non-Christian religions and the replacement of the existing cultures were almost goals for missionary work.

Such a change in the perception of values is drastic and will have tremendous consequences on the ways the mission will be conducted in the world. The insistence on the qualitative aspect means an attention to the cultures, which are collective phenomena, and a work which will not only respect the existing cultures (with the necessary critical position that the Church must have towards all cultures) but will try to help these cultures play more fully their role in mankind and in the Church. Therefore not only a systematic knowledge of the cultures will be necessary, but also a whole new approach. To add numerical conversions to a "ghetto" church in an Asian country will make very little difference for the work of salvation, if this is not done in accordance with the new perspectives.

Such a change is traumatic for some of the "missionary churches." Their identification in their own society has been precisely to be distinct from it, "to be others." They feel lost in a pagan ocean if they must lose their signs of identity, which are generally Western. In India, for example, the efforts of adaptation to Indian art in liturgical buildings and functions are now more encouraged by foreign missionaries than by the Indians themselves. Is this not a sign of some "religious alienation"?

The new emphasis given to a more qualitative understanding of the mission is disturbing very profoundly the whole definition of the work and the apostolate of the missionaries. It is often painful to see how the changes are affecting some of the older priests. Some are bewildered and others have become very much discouraged, feeling that all their earlier work has counted for nothing. A few think that the emphasis on a qualitative approach means that the Church is simply abandoning her mission to all men and devoting herself to an elite. And still others are calling for a halt in missionary activity to give time and thought to redefining ends and means.

So this is a period of great difficulty, of confusion, and of some crises for the missionary congregations. The outcome will depend very much on the attitudes and directions taken by the superiors or provincials in missionary work in training and retraining their members. It is a hopeful sign that some are taking the changes extremely well and are going through a whole retraining period to help themselves to adapt their vision of the Church to that of the conciliar documents.

This is true of some congregations, for example, in Africa where it is especially needed and where political events are serving to hasten the change. The missions can no longer depend upon financial support or subsidies from colonial powers. The status of the missions in society is no longer the same in those African countries which have achieved independence.

But while this is a time of difficulty for the missions, it is also a time of hope. Efforts to study the problems are bringing some congregations closer together and providing opportunities for closer and much-needed cooperation and exchange of experience and ideas. For example, the White Fathers and the Congregation of African Missions are now working so closely together that when one superior general visits missionaries of his congregation he makes a visit to the missionaries of the other congregation in the name of their superior. This in itself has relatively little significance unless it is known that before the Council many congregations were generally rather exclusive and almost jealously concerned about maintaining their "identity."

Not only has the renewed understanding of the Church as the people of God resulted in a new approach to those non-Western cultures outside the Church, it has resulted also in the rediscovery of the missionary aspect in our so-called "Christian Western civilization."

We are living in what has been called the "post-Christian" era. Even though we have a physical institutional presence of the Church in terms of numbers of parishes, schools, hospitals and so on, many people are non-believers. There is very little communication between the Church and members of the "sub-cultures" in our society: scientists, laborers, artists, physicians, intellectuals, politicians, and so on. What little there is exists almost by accident and is not very well understood or supported by the whole Church. This has been one of the great problems of the worker-priests in France, for example.

The motivation for this specialized apostolate was sound because it was based on a recognition that the Church had "lost" the working class and that there was a need for a special apostolate among the workers. But as it was carried out it became less a witness of the presence of the Church among the workers (for various reasons), and more the witness of the presence of individual isolated priests. And this resulted in many problems and conflicts which led eventually to the suspension of the worker-priests in France. In Belgium this apostolate has continued now for almost twenty years, and it has recently been taken up again in France.

But in order for these specialized apostolates to be effective, their witness must be seen as a common effort of the whole community, as having the support of the whole people of God. It should be known that it is not just a matter of one isolated priest being involved in the effort, or even a particular group of priests, but that these priests are in full solidarity with the whole Church and have the support of their bishop and of all the parishes. And this must be shown in a very concrete way. Then the apostolate will be seen as a witness of the collective presence of the Church in this particular sphere, and not of just one or two "far-out" members of the clergy whose influence on the rest of the clergy may actually be quite marginal.

I don't say that the only way to meet these sub-cultures is to have priests working as scientists, laborers, in inter-racial work, and so on, but if we want to actualize the presence of Christ in all these "worlds" we must develop some means of communication with them other than the traditional ones. It is not generally true that in the world of the parish these other worlds will be encountered or influenced automatically.

What is more likely to happen is that the separation will be internal, compartmentalized: the life of worship in the parish and the message of the Gospel will not be related to the life of action and work in the world. And this kind of separation of the Gospel from the workaday world is in some ways much worse than a complete ab-sence of the Gospel because it permits a man to think of himself as a Christian while at the same time living his life entirely outside Christian orientations. Instead of giv-ing *no* witness, he is giving a *false* witness. We have only to look at the actions of supposedly Christian nations in recent history to see that Christian values have not been noticeably present in our relations with one another.

The very fact, for example, that about 90% of the population in the countries of Latin America is baptized Catholic and that Catholicism is taken for granted as part of the whole culture makes a re-examination for quality more difficult. It is necessary, however, because the whole social situation which prevails in most of these countries testifies to the fact that Christian values are absent from the organization of social life. And in countries which are nominally 90% Catholic this fact says something about the quality of their evangelization.

A whole re-examination is needed, and it will be met by resistance. It does not take much of a prophet to say this. There are some bishops and priests in some Latin American countries who are leading figures in the fight for social reform, however. This fact is causing real amazement in some of the Communist countries I have visited because they never thought to see the Church involved in these matters. Some Marxist intellectuals are even beginning to revise their ideas about religion.

The encyclicals of Pope John XXIII, *Pacem in Terris* and *Mater et Magistra,* the documents of the Council, especially the Constitution on the Church in the Modern World, and Pope Paul's encyclical, *Populorum Progressio,* are giving rise to many questions about the Church. During a visit to Moscow I talked for more than an hour with the president and the secretary of the Academy of Science, and our conversation was about the Council and the Popes' encyclicals. They really wondered to see the Church so concerned with the problems of this world and with their just solution. It was a new fact for them, which did not fit in with their traditional view of the role of religion.

But we must always be aware that this qualitative mission will be a source of constant tension in the Church because we are involved in the paradoxical situation of creating an identification, an assimilation of culture, in any given country without actually identifying with it to the exclusion of other groups, or peoples, or cultures. It is a delicate balance to maintain. And it is one which can be just as difficult to maintain in parishes and with small groups. The temptation is always present to create a new culture, a separate people, an "in" group. But this is not desirable for the mission of the Church, either in the world, or in a country, or in a parish, because it creates small closed societies and is contrary to the Church's witness of universal acceptance.

The Council opened for the whole Church this new approach to evangelization: to announce salvation in a Savior already present and acting in the whole world and to invite all peoples to an assembly which, while not constituting a separate "people" culturally defined like the races of the earth, nevertheless has a visible existence

and is characterized by a permanent reference to a revealed God, expressed in prayer and worship and in
criteria of action in the world. This is a Church com-
patible with all human cultures and societies. In the
theological sphere this is nothing new, but the reality of
the life of the Roman Catholic Church was quite different from this model. The identification with a culture,
the Western culture, even if denied in "essence," was a
fact in "existence."

Of course we will never have a completely "pure ecclesiastical community" because the message of Christ is
communicated through the fabric of the different cultures, and to sustain such a position would be to refuse
an incarnated Church. But we have to tend toward a
really universal community of mankind—only perfectly
realized in Christ at the time of the *parousia*—and therefore use all the existing channels of human communication in their ever changing reality.

We spoke also of a third external aim: to act in the
world in terms of the Gospel. Here, too, we notice a
fundamental change brought by the Council. *Gaudium
et Spes* reversed our vision of the world. We may say that
this is the first official and radical transformation of attitude in the Church since the birth of scientific civilization. And since the mission of the Church is to be the
sacrament of Christ in the world, it matters very greatly
how the Church perceives the "world." This perception
will be very much linked with the understanding she has

of her own aims and of how these are related to all her ways of action and work in the world.

The Council has given the Church a new and different orientation to the world. The old view saw the world as hostile to the Church and the Church as hostile to the world. A complete withdrawal from the world was encouraged, and a life of the Church centered upon herself without any relevance to the world or communication with the world developed. This "detachment" was expressed almost as a doctrine, and a spirituality of withdrawal from the world was preached as the ideal.

Of course this resulted in a lack of acceptance of social responsibility and created, in a certain way, a schizophrenic religion, especially among the wealthier members of the Church. In one European country an industrialist receiving the Eucharist often was called an "eater of hosts" because he was so completely unaware of any social responsibility. And in Latin American countries some very "pious" landowners, having thousands of acres, will strongly oppose all land reform, so necessary for development. But because their "spirituality" is so unrelated to this world they feel completely justified in continuing this unjust system, together with a life of prayer and sacraments.

The Council, however, clearly put an accent on man's social responsibility in building up the world. The Constitution on the Church in the Modern World was based on a biblical vision of the world, not identifying the world with sin, although evil exists in the world, but seeing it as created by God and given in stewardship to man.

It was very difficult for some bishops to accept the necessity for the Church to reflect on temporal realities, to find out the facts and to take into account the changing conditions of man's existence before making moral pronouncements about them. But after a great deal of discussion (there were 23,000 amendments to Schema 13, almost one for each word!) the vision of the world within which the Church is to work was clarified. This world is seen to be a world in the process of technological development, with new relations between man and nature and new relations between man and man; a world that is interdependent, pluralistic, urban, mobile, specialized, socialized, secularized, and in an ever accelerating process of rapid and continuing social change; a world with an increased awareness of human values, of the dignity of the human person and a consciousness that freedom is necessary for the pursuit of goodness; a world which possesses the means to solve mankind's problems of hunger, disease, and want as well as the means to destroy all of man's progress; a world in which the Spirit is already at work and a world in need of an encounter with Christ.

However, the role of the Church in this world is not to build another Christendom on a global scale, or to attempt to create small or partial Christendoms in one country or in one institution. All the Council documents make this clear. The Church seeks no temporal power in the world.

The fact that the Church in Council directed herself to involvement in man's human condition is an acknowledgment that she has not always been immersed in history in this sense. Her role in political life went from one of too much power to one of too great detachment. It is now necessary for her to work out a new role, not the one of domination exercised in medieval times nor the one of withdrawal practiced in recent centuries, but one of orientation. The role of the Church in the world today is a prophetic role: to recognize the legitimate aims of man in a changing world and to give concrete orientations that will be conducive to the unity of men in peace and justice.

The perception of a new relationship between the Church and the world will bring about changes in the Church not only in her ways of thinking about the world —and the documents on the Church in the Modern World, on Religious Freedom, and on the Non-Christian Religions are certainly quite different from the way Pope Pius IX would have written them—but also changes in her approaches to the world.

A new awareness of the condition of man based on fact and not on outdated theory will be reflected in moral theology if we are really serious in giving an orientation to men of this time. Moral theology has to apply changing concepts of man and the teaching of the Gospel to the concrete situation of man. This is why a sociological approach is always helpful to moral theology because it helps us to know *what* the concrete situation of man *is*.

We are living in a dynamic society where responsibility rests more and more with the person. The old concept that the Church can give *all* the moral guidance does not fit the facts of today. But the Church does have a responsibility for addressing herself to the great problems of peace and social development, which are taking on new and more crucial dimensions in the world today. And that is why it is so important for theologians to be working on the problems of tomorrow, not only those of today.

Christians cannot suspend action in their lives to await the judgment of theologians. Birth control, for example, is already a very old problem; the problem of tomorrow is the control of genetics. But if the Church just ignores all these foreseeable developments or automatically reacts in a negative fashion, she cannot really claim to be fulfilling her mission to be "the light of nations." The world will look elsewhere for its light.

I suppose we could say that from an ultimate standpoint we don't have to be too much concerned about whether the great orientations to mankind come from within or from outside the Church, because the history of salvation is the history of man and God is present in this one reality. Even if the institutional Church should lag behind, God remains the Lord of history. But from a proximate standpoint we must be very much concerned because we, the Church, the people of God, have been given the responsibility of being the vehicle of Christ to the world. To be faithful to this mission the Church must be attentive to the "signs of the times" in order to be able to interpret them in the spirit of the Gospel. The Commission on Justice and Peace has been created (not without resistance) in the central organization of the Church. If it has enough liberty of action, it can be a very useful instrument for creating such a consciousness among Christians.

Too often in history, as the Council Fathers acknowledged, the Church has not acted in accord with the spirit of the Gospel and has sometimes even been in opposition to it. With the self-understanding that has arisen in the Church and has been communicated to the world by means of the Council documents, there is no excuse for us if we do not respond to the great needs of mankind today.

If we really take the world seriously, as the Council has urged us to do, we will be unable to continue with our ecclesiastical institutions just as they are. We will be morally forced to re-examine them, looking at them from outside, to see how well they are fulfilling the mission of the Church to the world. We must, therefore, use a systematic approach to find out what the needs are. A few years ago the United Nations proposed to give to the

Vatican the complete series of UN publications—those of
the Food and Agricultural Organization, the World
Health Organization, the International Labor Organization, and so on. But the Vatican rejected the offer. No
machinery existed to handle this literature. But this is
needed documentation; lacking such information, we will
always be too late and will become increasingly irrelevant. We need a new structure in the Church to work
with this information on a permanent level if we are to
take the world problem of underdevelopment seriously.
What we need is not good will, because good will is
there. We must give adequate help and work with facts
and imagination to effect a real solution to these problems.

Setting up small "microrealizations" is not enough; this
does little to change the overall situation. Changes must
be very fundamental. It does little good for the Church
to finance small isolated schools or to maintain "model"
agricultural cooperatives. This could only give us the illusion that we are helping. I do not mean that the world
has no need for "prophetic gestures" on the part of the
Church. These are very necessary and very important.
But in conjunction with these, the Church must work
towards broad social reforms and support the legitimate
aspirations of the people even if this leads, sometimes, to
revolution.

Of course, I am not saying anything new. The Constitution on the Church in the Modern World said the same

thing and Pope Paul's recent encyclical on the Development of Peoples repeated it. But it is one thing to support on paper the necessity for a social revolution in certain circumstances, and quite another to recognize the need when it actually arises.

We have seen an example of this just recently in the case of Camilo Torres in Colombia. To make an analysis of Father Torres' decision to participate in guerilla warfare, it is first necessary to discuss briefly the situation of the Church and of society in Colombia.

Colombia had a very closed type of social structure, almost feudal, and the Church was linked with that structure. Very little social change had been accomplished over the years. The Church was generally conservative and the clergy quite authoritarian, especially in the rural areas. Pastoral work, for the most part, was conceived in terms of assuring the prestige and strength of the Church, with a deeply ritualistic approach to religion. The priest, especially in small rural villages, was about the only recognized leader.

The country has had a long history of internal violence. There were 300,000 persons killed between 1948 and 1958, and there is still intermittent guerilla warfare even though a truce was established between the Liberal and Conservative parties in 1957, when dictator Rojas Pinilla was overthrown. A coalition government of Liberals and Conservatives was formed at that time to rule jointly for twelve years, and this government has been relatively stable. But no real change in the social structure of the country was made and the unrest was growing. The Church during this time was very much involved in schools, universities, and orphanages but had done little to help change the social structure.

I first met Camilo Torres in 1954 when I gave a conference at his seminary. At that time he was a member of a small group of seminarians studying social problems. He was older than most of the other young men of his country when he entered the seminary, about nineteen or twenty.

After his ordination he came to study at Louvain. When he returned to his own country after having been away for four years, he really saw the situation there with "other eyes." And it was a great shock. He was first assigned as a chaplain at the national University in Bogotá and then took a job as professor of sociology there because he thought it was better for his work as a priest to be a professor rather than a chaplain who, in the eyes of the students, was expected to act as a sort of watch dog to keep them quiet.

He became quite influential with the students, and during a period of strikes they elected him rector of the University—which was really remarkable because the students are generally very anti-clerical. But this was too much for the Church officials and he was relieved of his position and made a curate in a parish. Then he was dean of studies at the administrative school of the state.

During all this time he was trying to work in the Church but, to his mind, this had little effect because the Church was too closely linked with the existing social structures.

Finally Torres asked to be "reduced" to lay status. (I really hope this word will be changed!) He wrote a letter explaining why he asked this, expressing his conviction that in such circumstances to say Mass without working for social justice was just a lie, because we had to prove our love for people before offering the sacrifice. But his position was not understood. There was an exchange of letters in the press between the Cardinal and Father Torres, but no dialogue. He did not reject the faith or his priesthood. He asked to be relieved of the functions of the priesthood with the hope of being able some day again to celebrate the Mass.

He had hoped to build a popular movement which could bring about a bloodless revolution, but he was quite naive politically and not much of an organizer. At first the Communists tried to make use of his movement, but this did not last very long. He was advised to leave the country; his life was in danger because of his political positions. And he could have gone many places in the world because he had many friends. But he thought that to do this would be to abandon the people who had looked to him for leadership.

His movement began in March of 1965, in December of that year he joined the guerillas, and he was killed in

February, 1966. There was very little political reaction at first, but since that time small groups of students calling themselves "Camilista" have been forming among the students to continue to work for social reform. In July of 1966 some Colombian bishops issued two documents on pastoral action of the Church and on the social situation in Colombia, using very strong words, and Camilo Torres' death may have been partly responsible for this action.

There have been some very adverse reactions to what this man has done, some people saying that he should never have been ordained a priest. But rather than looking on Camilo Torres as an "ex-priest," why not recognize that his life was a prophetic witness in the development of the society in which he was living? I am not saying it was the only type of witness possible and I am not advocating guerilla warfare as the solution, but we must work urgently at creating new structures in the Church to meet the new needs in the world. And this is even more urgent in those countries where the Church has, because of historical reasons, a position of social influence.

Not only must we work at creating new structures to meet new needs, we must also transform or completely abandon old structures which are not really witnessing to Christ in the world today. If we just conserve all the institutions and practices which have accumulated during the centuries we will not be a witness to Christ, but just a living museum of the Holy Roman Empire, the Middle

Ages, and the High Renaissance. The Council stressed the role of the Church as a *servant* in the world and not as a power. But we are still burdened with many of the trappings of power and prestige and do not seem to be in very much of a hurry to get rid of them.

The transformation in the way of realizing the mission of the Church in the world had been developing for some time before the Council but was, I would say, "legitimized" by the Council. The new view will take some time to be applied, however. The reaction of the Protestant observers at the Council to the attitudes expressed in these documents was very favorable, but they asked: "Will we see that? Visibly?" So it is not just a matter of verbally renouncing a position of political power and social prestige. We must take a good hard look at our actual behavior and image in the world and see where we must change.

How can the Church call herself the servant of mankind when she is installed in palaces even in the poorest countries? This is truly a scandal. And it is not merely a question of waiting, for the outward signs to change, until old buildings wear themselves out, because elaborate buildings are being bought or constructed even today.

And there are other forms of prestige. Just before the war, Msgr. Cardijn had been received at lunch by a bishop in Yugoslavia, and he was horrified by the experience. There was a servant for each person standing be-

hind each chair throughout the whole meal. It was as if
this were the court of a Renaissance duke. A few years
later the reality was a little different!

In American society the sign of prestige is expressed in
dollars, and many diocesan papers in the United States
reveal the success story in terms of the costs of buildings:
schools, churches, rectories, convents, and the like. This
is not necessarily a sign of materialism, as is thought by
those outside the country, so much as it is regarded as a
sign of success and therefore a matter of prestige: of being successful in a successful society in order to be fully
accepted by it. The assimiliation of the middle-class
values has succeeded perhaps too well, and it may be
only when the meaning behind the protest of the "hip-
pies" is understood that more evangelical values will be
rediscovered.

Protests have been made in the Church before about
signs of prestige and power, but what is new is that we
now have a pastoral constitution rejecting these signs of
outward pomp and display. The problem is not solved by
a text, but at least we have a solid base for a re-orienta-
tion. *Gaudium et Spes* is a most revolutionary document,
but the great temptation is to use it as a verbal monu-
ment too precious to be approached and to put an inscrip-
tion before it, as in a museum: "Please don't touch"!

The Council has also rejected what was at one time in
the history of the Church an ideal: the confessional state.
Now separation of Church and State is seen as the model.

A few archaic situations still remain in some countries, but as a whole the problem is now solved.

So, in a word, the Constitution on the Church in the Modern World made us accept the world as a secular reality, put by God at the disposal of man for the development of humanity. It pointed to the meaning of the construction of this world for the Kingdom of God and, indicating that this Kingdom is not of this world; it said clearly that there is a mysterious link between this earth and the "new creation" and that what man makes of this world is not indifferent to the next one.

Such an affirmation of the value of the world is really more explosive than any declaration on family morals or on war and peace contained in the same document. It means that the task of the Christian is in the world. It means that the church is not a society in itself. It means that the Church is a servant in the world, servant of God and of man. It means that the Church, being the sign of God and the sign of the unity of mankind in the world (*Lumen Gentium*), must express this outwardly in a language which is understood by man in the world. We need time to come to the full acknowledgment of such a truth and even more time to come to the concrete consequences of this truth in the life of the Church.

The full acceptance of a secularized world in the life of every Christian means that the very first place of encounter with God is in the world of men. It is in a world where he exercises a full responsibility that man can be said to be really created in the image of God. It is in the world that Christ is active through the Holy Spirit. It is in the world that man is preparing the new creation. And all this receives its full meaning in worship and, more particularly, in the Eucharist, which not only signifies but already actualizes the union with God and the unity of all men.

The Church's institution is only a service of man in the world, and not a specific "world." It must correspond to the reality it is intended to symbolize and always try to express in the most intelligible way for men of every culture and of every society the union with God and the unity of all mankind. This expression will call for a profound and permanent revision of the structures of the Church herself and of the relations between the Church as institution and the temporal realities.

Internal Aims: A Community of Believers

It is not difficult to see that a change of emphasis in the external aims of the Church will be reflected in the internal aims, because these aims are really one and are divisible only for discussion.

The accent on participation has put more emphasis on the sense of belonging, of personal commitment, of personal responsibility for one's religious behavior, and less emphasis on forms of social control and external cohesion exercised by the clergy in order to achieve the internal aims of the Church: *internalization of values* and *the cohesion of the group.*

The first of these internal aims is an enduring aim, one which will not be accomplished once and for all. The internalization of values is to grow and become more profound as each person deepens his understanding and knowledge of God's message of salvation.

The real mission of the Church as institution is to make of every member of the people of God a *conscious* member of the people of God. It is not to build schools, or hospitals, or imposing complexes of "religious" institutions. It is to build up conscious membership in the people of God, enabling them to live in conscious accord with Christian values of faith and love.

The cohesion of the group is also a continuing aim because we are called not only to an individual faith but to an assembly. The Church is the people of God, and if this is to be a visible assembly there will necessarily have to be some institutionalization, not to immobilize the group but to keep it together as a people.

Such practices by some isolated pastors, for example, as refusing to lead services at a wake unless the deceased has been a member of the parish "Holy Name Society" or the "Altar and Rosary Society" are recognized to be a positively indefensible form of "social control." The same is true of the practice by some teaching nuns of requiring a child to bring a note from the parents telling his whereabouts if he failed to attend the children's Mass on Sunday. These are things of the past—at least I certainly hope so—but they were practiced by some as a form of social control on the part of the "institutional" Church to bring about an external conformity of behavior to what should have been an expression of an internal motivation based on faith and love.

Now it is recognized—at least in the documents of the Council—that personal adherence to the Church is to be the goal of the pastoral care rather than a cultural adherence or an external "policing" by the institutional Church.

The presentation of the sacraments until the last few years (and in many places, *still*) has been excessively centered on an almost *automatic* efficacy of the sacraments in the lives of those receiving them. So much stress has been placed on the *"ex opere operato"* teaching concerning the sacraments that relatively little emphasis has been given to the person's faith as condition for receiving them. We have insisted so much that the sacrament of marriage, for example, "confers" all the grace needed for this demanding state of adult Christian living that we have neglected to stress that personal preparation and mature awareness of the responsibilities and meaning of conjugal love are needed as well. In other words, we priests have almost regarded our "work" as complete if we have "administered" the sacraments—we could depend on God's grace to take care of all the rest!

The growing awareness that receiving the sacraments

is an *expression* of a personal faith and commitment is leading to a real change in the pastoral preparation for their reception. Already important changes have been made in the quality of marriage preparation offered in those places where the Pre-Cana and Cana movements are well established under competent and well-trained directors, but the time will come when we will see that the serious preparation for marriage must be *required* rather than optional, and when counseling both before and after marriage is provided on a professional level as part of our pastoral care. This, of course, does not mean that this care will be provided only by priests.

More personal preparation for the reception of the sacrament of the Eucharist is also being stressed in some dioceses, where the parents prepare their children to receive this sacrament with assistance from priests, sisters, or other laymen. The readiness of the child in terms of his own faith and understanding is the basis for determining when he shall receive this sacrament rather than an arbitrary date or chronological age chosen for a whole class to receive.

This practice puts greater emphasis on the development of a personal faith and commitment from the standpoint of both the parents and the child and tends to give additional emphasis to the concept of responsible parenthood.

In the openings made by the Council, there is a trend of putting more and more responsibility onto the persons themselves. The accent is put on personal responsibility for moral behavior and a recognition that it is not the role of the Church to give a "catalog" of acceptable moral behavior for each and every circumstance in one's life. This trend is especially evident in the Dogmatic Constitution on the Church, the Pastoral Constitution on the Church in the Modern World, the Declaration on Religious Freedom, and the Decree on the Lay Apostolate, but it is implicit in other documents as well.

The recognition that the lay apostolate *rests on baptism* and not on a mandate given by the bishop is another indication of the trend to emphasize personal responsibility. The old idea was that the lay apostolate was an extension of the apostolate of the hierarchy. This was based on the concept that the "apostolate" was reserved for priests, but since there were not enough priests to go around, the mandate was extended to include some lay people.

The new interpretation of the lay apostolate does not exclude some *movements* as being given a mandate by the bishop to act collectively in the name of the Church as institution, but the definition of the Church as the people of God means that the mission of the Church belongs to each member in a very special way and that his participation in the life of the Church is not a privilege but a right and a duty.

So the necessity for forming Christians able to live this kind of responsible life in the Church and in the world is little by little leading to a new view of pastoral work within the Church. This view is based on the personal responsibility of informed Christian people and a greater participation of the people in the actual organization of structures in the Church.

The new understanding of the external and internal aims of the Church in relation to a new perception of the world has established a background for the action of the Church. This will call for a qualitative approach to both men and nations, an attitude of service, and an emphasis on the participation of all the people of God in the life of the Church and of the world.

2 A VANISHING OR A TRANSFORMING INSTITUTION?

In order to translate all these insights of the Council into actuality, we must expect a real tranformation in *roles,* in some institutional *structures,* and in our *relations with other groups and religions* in society. The organizational consequences of all these transformations will be very great.

If the Council had changed only some organizational aspects of the life of the Church, even very important ones, some isolated reactions might have followed and perhaps even some separation, as, for example, the Old Catholics after Vatican I. But the work of Vatican II is more comprehensive. Cardinal Suenens, archbishop of Malines-Brussels, declared at a theological Congress held in Toronto that Vatican II put an end to several periods in the life of the Catholic Church. It put an end to the Constantinian era and brought to a close the era of the Counter-Reformation. And this is true. We could add that it also put an end to the Scholastic era and to the era of Anti-Modernism. And even if we have to admit that such affirmations are a little too simplistic, we must conclude that the work of Vatican II is a real revolution. If this is true, and it is, we should not be surprised at the present state of turmoil in the Church, for nobody expects a revolution to happen without any troubles or disorder.

When an institution revises its definition of itself and reformulates its external and internal goals, even if it does not at the same time change its organizational aspects, these will still have to go through a complete revision. This is what is happening in the Church today. The revision made by the Council is such that we may not expect any aspect of her organization to remain immune from profound reform. And of course this is not a comfortable situation. The Council performed such a revision only for some roles and institutions, however, leaving for the post-conciliar period the concrete realization of what this implied.

Because the Council was so little expected and because many were wholly unprepared to absorb, in such a short period, so considerable a shock, present reactions and tensions are inevitable. The churches in some areas, better prepared, are managing to go through the post-conciliar period without major crises. Others, coming very rapidly out of a period of authoritarian organization and closed thinking, are experiencing greater difficulties.

But it would be a complete illusion to think that we are

coming to the end of the changes in the Church. Some
think that it is time now to put an end to this turmoil,
and we hear so many warnings about the necessity of
respecting venerable traditions, of coming back to traditional formulations, of the virtue of obedience, and the
like. Cardinal Suenens at the same theological meeting at
Toronto said: "Pope John said that we are living in a
springtime of the Church. But the spring in our hemi-
sphere may come in March, in April or in May. We are in
March. It is an early spring, with heavy rains and even
snow and freezing during the night." In other words, the
Council did not achieve renewal in the Church; it made
only a beginning.

It is true that the problems raised in the Church today
are more profound than just questions of reorganization.
This is because we are facing not only a structural
change, but also a deep cultural change. By this I mean
that the formulation of the faith itself is involved. There
is in the secularization process the danger, as Harvey Cox
puts it, of "secularism," which means the total "evacua-
tion" of God. There is in the theology of "the death of
God" the possibility of fundamental atheism.

But there is also the danger, in all the reactions against
such currents, of refusing to look at the facts. And these
facts are that we are living in the midst of a cultural mu-
tation of mankind, where the developments in theology
and the scientific study of scripture, limited in the past
largely to the province of scholars, have passed to the

popular level and form the prevailing attitude. The faith
is in danger, yes. But it is not by stressing a fidelity to
formulations which no longer speak to the mentality of
modern man and making faith a matter of obedience to
the authority of the ecclesiastical power structure that we
shall solve the problem.

The fact remains that faith is transmitted by the word,
and salvation comes through the Church. This involves a
twofold problem. For whatever the difficulties presented
by the "explosion of language" we are facing today, a language must be found in which the immutable truths can
be conveyed to men. And whatever the direction our
critique of the Church takes, it must not lead us in the
direction of the "angelical" vision of an assembly without
structures and organization, a social body free of any
time lag.

The faith will be in even greater danger, however, from
irresponsibility from either of two extremes—theologians
who act recklessly with regard to the community of the
faithful or Church authorities who try to stop thinking in
the Church and obstruct the necessary changes in ecclesiastical structures.

Of course we are living in difficult times. Such times
require a deep sense of the Church. This means a deep
sense of her mission in the world, which is to be the sign
of the God who is and of the God who comes and also to
be the sign of the unity of all mankind.

So, as we have said, to translate all these perceptions of

the Council into reality, we can expect to see a transformation in roles, in institutions, and in our relations with other groups and religions.

ROLES: IN PARTICULAR, THE PRIEST

Before we discuss what is happening to the role of the priest, it may be useful to elaborate somewhat the definition of "role."

What is the meaning of role? The word was first used to designate a piece of papyrus which was *rolled*. From that came the word "roll" meaning "register." This word was also applied to the theater—the "role" on paper—and from this came the present use of the word "role" to indicate the duties we have to perform in the theater of the world.

We know there are basic needs in each society—political, family, educational, economic, leisure, religious. These are universal needs and all societies must provide for them. Society must organize functions to meet these needs, and these functions are administered by groups. The more complex the society, the more specialized are the groups. Some hierarchy is needed for each organized function, some structure determining what is expected from each *role*.

Almost all roles have a certain "status" attached to

them. A person must perform a role; the status attached to the role exists in the minds of other people in terms of expectations and recognition. The role is what one must do to live up to the expectations of the society in which it is performed.

Status is much more complex than role. It is very much linked with social and cultural changes, changes in the values of the society. Status is not necessarily related to the objective importance of the role. Some roles are very necessary, but in some countries their status is not very high, for example, the status of nurse or teacher. Some societies rank the same profession higher or lower according to their cultural values.

The same is true of the status of the priest. In a theocracy his status will be very high; in a secular society it may not rank so high. When the priesthood is high in status there are more vocations. When the status is low, there are fewer vocations, but perhaps the motivations are better because when the status of the priesthood is high there may be a variety of social motivations as well as religious. Status tends to be reinforced by external signs such as a title and a special form of dress.

There are two forms of status: *assigned* and *acquired.* An assigned status is one which is automatically conferred with a function, and this type is predominant in a closed society. An acquired status is one which is achieved through personal effort and is more typical of a democratic society, a "meritocracy."

The status of the priest in the Church is becoming more acquired than automatic because we are living in a society where the acquired type of status is more developed. This will mean a change for the priest because many have expected a high status just because they were priests.

Some signs of priestly status will simply seem remnants of the past and should be allowed to disappear: titles such as "monsignor" and some symbols of office such as the miter and crosier, as well as the ornate robes of the Renaissance. The Russian Orthodox priest still thinks he should have a beard and long hair in order to have the status of a priest, and in Africa the missionaries can be almost divided by sight into traditional or modern according to whether or not they are wearing beards. (Maybe the beard is not the best example—it enjoys periodic revivals!)

So status is more complex than role, and though it may not greatly affect the exercise of the role objectively speaking, it may have some psychological effects.

Roles are relative. For example, if there is a teacher, there are students. Society has established a model for the role; each person does not make the model himself. But the model differs very much from one culture to another. The role of an American housewife is very different, for example, from that of an Italian housewife. While the function itself may be in many aspects universal and determines the role to some extent, still the way a housewife fulfills this function will be regulated by the culture in which she is living.

There is always some possibility, however, for personal expression, for some liberty, except in extremely limited and very clearly defined roles such as, for example, someone marching in a parade. But on the whole we do not have to perform our roles in society as soldiers marching in a parade!

The same is true of the priest. The Church defines the primary function, but the way it can be fulfilled by each priest will depend greatly on the culture in which he is to exercise this function.

For example, in Europe for a priest to play golf would be almost incompatible with his role; in America it is almost a sign of being a priest! I am exaggerating, of course, but in Europe there is just no space for many golf courses, and the game is played only by the very, very wealthy. There is a certain freedom of action, then, in the performance of the role of priest, but it will be somewhat circumscribed according to the culture. The example given is quite peripheral, but the same principle is true for more fundamental aspects, such as work, marriage, and so on.

All of us have many roles, but each of us has what is called a *key* role. This is the role by which you define yourself, or which is assigned to you by society, and it is usually the professional role. And there are times when these roles conflict.

Conflicts can be external or internal. External conflicts of role occur between persons when the roles are ill-defined, and this often happens during a time of change. Or the conflict can be internal, between two or more roles within one person, for example, the priest-teacher.

What is happening, then, to the role of the priest in this time of change in the Church and in the world?

Because of the new accents put on the functions in the Church by the Council—pastoral, sacramental, cultural, missionary—there will consequently be a change in the roles centered around such functions.

For example: If the function of the parish is to try to keep some cohesion in this group of people baptized in the Catholic Church through the exercise of a strong and an almost exclusive leadership by the priest, as a means of assuring a social control and keeping these people together as a group, this will lead to one type of definition of the role of the priest.

But if the function of the parish is to allow the constitution of a community of people believing in Jesus Christ, based not so much on a compulsory belonging such as the one determined by a certain territory but more on some kind of choice and motivated by faith, to actualize the Eucharistic community, then the role of the priest will be defined in another way. His leadership will be manifested much more in his capacity for education than in his administrative ability. It will not be an exclusive type of leadership, but one which will consist in sharing decisions and control not only with other priests but with lay people also.

The emphasis put on the active participation of the people in the liturgy, for example, will require that they share in the responsibility for its celebration. The priest will not be able really to create a Eucharistic community, at least from a psychological and social standpoint, if he does not relinquish some of his exclusive control over this central act of Christian life and worship and involve the people in participation through shared responsibility and education.

These changes in the role of the priest are implicit in the new vision of the Church, but the Council also made some explicit changes in roles. This is especially true of the role of the bishop. The bishop is now seen much more in his role as pastor than as administrator. With the Council's definition on collegiality he assumes a greater role of leadership and responsibility in the universal Church, while at the same time his role of exclusive jurisdiction and autonomy in the diocese is now to be shared with the national conference of bishops. His intervention in parish affairs will be more on a pastoral than an authoritarian level, and he is requested to establish a senate of priests, the *presbyterium,* and a pastoral council including lay people to consult with them and to assist him in fulfilling his pastoral function.

Roles are relative, as we said before; they exist in relation to other roles and functions. Because this is so, a change in the definition of one role or function will have an immediate effect on all the other roles and functions related to the one changed.

The Council did not make explicit changes in the role of the priest. Most of the specific changes were related to the role of the bishop and to the functions in the Church. But the role of the priest is being transformed, nevertheless, as we have seen in the example concerning the function of the parish.

We are experiencing a period of difficulty today in the working out of new roles because many priests do not understand the new role performance expected of them. This uncertainty contributes to a feeling of insecurity, together with all the varying types of personality reactions which accompany this feeling. And this is normal.

Role expectations are today very different, so different in fact as to be sometimes contradictory. Before the Council the great majority of priests and laymen shared the same expectations and understanding of the role of the priest. Both were generally united in their view of the priest as the leader, the authority in all religious matters, a sort of pope in his own parish.

This unanimity of understanding exists no longer. Of course not all of this change is due immediately to the Council. The Council legitimized and formally accepted many ideas and currents which were already present in the Church. The understanding of the role of the priest was already changing according to different places, groups, levels of education, theological training, and so on. Some priests and laymen were thinking in tune with the Council before the Council ever started and, as a result, accepted the new vision of the Church and their role in it with enthusiasm and real understanding.

But for those priests and people whose understanding has not changed either before or during or since the Council, the present situation is very difficult. It is made all the more difficult because some of the bishops and priests who are in positions to implement needed change in their dioceses, or parishes, or seminaries have not grasped the thinking of the Council, or made it their own. Some say they are too old to change and some are in complete reaction against all the changes.

They are often, then, in conflict with the younger generation of priests, who appreciate the need for change and would like to see the norms clearly defined and established for all. In a way these younger priests are sometimes themselves expressing a pre-conciliar attitude in asking that the values endorsed by the Council be *imposed*. What we must all recognize is that the Council has given a direction for the future and that time will be needed before these values can be internalized. Even a bishop who is most progressive cannot simply impose progressive values upon the priests of his diocese.

If we ask ourselves, also, what are the changes brought by the transformation of social values, especially in an urban world, we can indicate some characteristics.

First of all, there is a *change in status* from assigned to acquired, so that the way in which a priest performs his role will have more to do with the respect he inspires than will the simple fact that he is a priest.

Next, there is a *transformation in the definition* of the role of the priest from a more or less expressive function ("father") to a more instrumental function. This is the main dilemma of the priest today. For many reasons he cannot really be a "father" today to his parishioners. The parish is too large. There are too many people moving in and out of the parish all the time. People come to his church from other parishes, and his parishioners go to other parish churches. Much time is taken up by administrative functions. People have jobs, so there is often no one at home when he does find time to call. The level of the average parishioner's education has risen, so that the priest is not looked up to as the only leader in his community, and the expansion of knowledge in his own calling is so great that he cannot keep up with all the latest work in catechetics, scriptural studies, moral theology, pastoral theology, marriage counseling. And so on.

So his role is no longer one of exclusive leadership, but is more a role which is a *part* of a function distributed among several priests. It can no longer be determined solely by geography, but should be defined also according to other norms.

Each priest should have a double function, especially in urban pastoral life. With a territorial function, he should also have a specialized function, covering the whole city or a section of the city for specialized work.

In each city or section of the city or in each diocese, one priest could be responsible for the liturgy, to see how the reform is progressing, to be available for consultation, etc.; another priest could be responsible for catechetics, another for youth, another for marriage counseling, another for the workers, another for the intellectuals, another for interracial work, and so on. This would allow a priest to concentrate his abilities and to become a specialist in his own field. This would also keep him from becoming too immersed in parochial problems and reducing the whole world to the limits of one parish. It would also give him a recognized status in a specialized society.

This type of distribution for pastoral care is of course based upon sociological knowledge of the type of civilization in which we are living and especially of the characteristics which make an urban society possible.

One of the main characteristics of urban life, for example, is that there are centers for certain activities: business, recreation, shopping, residential, industrial, and so on, and that people in the city are used to traveling back and forth to these centers as they have need. In a certain way it does not make sense for department stores to be grouped together, or for several movie theaters or restaurants to be within a few blocks of one another. It would seem more logical if these were "distributed" in a better proportion among all the neighborhoods. But there is a psychological aspect to urban life as well as a logical aspect. One of the values of urban life is choice, and this is more freely exercised when everything is brought together and centered in certain areas, giving the possibility of comparisons. And mobility, which is necessary for urban life, makes choice possible.

Pastoral care, too, has to be exercised along some of these lines. A catechetical center, for example, could be set up for the whole city, but not in each parish. It would be possible to have all the latest materials for catechetical work, a film library, books, reading rooms and places for discussion, with priests, sisters or lay people in charge.

Another example of urban pastoral care is the "telephone centers," telephone numbers that people can call at any time, anonymously if they wish, to ask questions and receive advice. In Brussels, for example, there are three lines operating, with a whole organization of priests, doctors, and psychologists who cooperate in this program. Many of the calls concern marriage cases. There are also numbers that can be called for urgent needs, for immediate help. Some Protestant churches are involved in this work also, and this could become a cooperative project.

So the priest's role is being transformed, and the Church must make use of all of these opportunities for expanding pastoral care.

The theological function of the priest is defined from his relation to the Eucharist. It is he who actualizes the Eucharist and makes possible the Eucharistic community.

And this will always be his primary function: to celebrate the Mass and to prepare and to prolong the community which is actualized by the Eucharist. This is the purpose of his preaching and teaching.

But from the sociological point of view the priest may be everything you can think of—a teacher, a laborer, an engineer, a scientist, a doctor, a social worker, a journalist, married or celibate in any of these roles—but not without criteria.

First, the motivation of a priest to accept any kind of role must be an apostolic motivation. That is, it should not be seen as a way of achieving personal status or recognition, but as a way of serving the general mission of the Church in accordance with his particular ability and talents.

Second, the priest should not seek to exert power, not that he need fear to assume the authority proper to his vocation (in any role there is some assumption of responsibility that is both normal and necessary), but that the seeking of power will bring him eventually into conflict with certain groups and make the exercise of his role of unifying the Eucharistic community harder.

What of the conflict which arises when a priest addresses himself in a prophetic way to social problems such as racial segregation, migrant workers, social reform, war and peace? This kind of conflict which is directly related to the mission of the Church cannot be avoided. But the reconciliation of all men in Christ is the constant aim of the Church, and the priest must keep this always in mind. He cannot forget that Christ came to save sinners as well as the "just men."

So the role of the priest in the modern world is undergoing a transformation and is changing from one of exclusive leadership in a parish to a collegial sharing of pastoral responsibility with other priests under the bishop. The process of transformation is a difficult one, but it is one which must be met and carried out everywhere in the Church.

With the change of emphasis in roles we are finding new problems in the recruitment and in the formation of seminarians.

In some seminaries the approach to the training of priests is still based on the orientation given by the Council of Trent. Contact with the world was supposed to be kept to a minimum, and this was, for example, one of the reasons why the majority of the seminaries were built in the country!

Not only is there an attempt to keep seminary training "out of this world," there is often little attention paid to the values of the world from which the seminarians have come. Young men entering the seminary today have grown up in a pluralistic, secularized world where modern values are accentuated—the value of freedom, the value of tolerance, the value of choice, the value of dialogue—values which are often in contradiction to the values established traditionally for the formation of priests. Is it surprising, then, that we are having a crisis in recruitment or that many young men are leaving the seminaries?

Actually many of the new values are endorsed by the Council, but the image of the priesthood formed in the minds of many young men too often does not conform to the reality of their personal experience.

The restoration of the diaconate on a permanent level presents another problem of definition of role. There are already experiments underway in Germany, France, and Brazil. Each country is emphasizing various aspects of the possibilities of the order of deacon, ranging from somewhat limited liturgical functions to almost complete pastoral care with the exception of saying Mass and hearing confessions. Careful study must be given to the definition of this role so that it does not appear so low in status as to seem to call for little more than a consecrated usher. Nor should it be seen as somehow the "coronation" of the lay apostolate. It is a special vocation, but one whose definition is not yet complete.

As a matter of fact very little has yet been concretely defined about the role of the priest. This is why we must expect in the future more reflections and more experiences. The article by Msgr. Ivan Illich in the June, 1967, issue of *The Critic* entitled "The Vanishing Clergyman" is a very typical expression of what is awaiting us in the months and the years to come.

It may well be that continued reflection and experience

will lead us in an unexpected direction, more radical than
we have thought even during the Council. But why fear
to face such a prospect? The most important fact is the
Christian vocation of all members of the people of God.
The exact way of exercising the ministry is secondary. In
a few years it is probable that there will be a great diversity of ministries, with a certain specialization of them:
some will be prophets, others will be teachers in the mysteries of God, some will baptize and others will govern
in the Church. And all these ministries will not necessarily be restricted to a full-time employee of the ecclesiastical organization, celibate and a member of a clerical
"caste." Would that be so extraordinary? I remember a
certain Paul . . .

The transition from the present situation toward one
as yet unknown will not be easy, but an inflexible enforcement of the present structures is not the best way of
helping all the people of God in such a period. To dream
of the future without facing up to the realities of the
present is not very wise either, but the responsibilities of
living in the present include the preparation of the future.

INSTITUTIONS: IN PARTICULAR, THE
PARISH

All the concrete institutions in the Church—which may
be described as *organized patterns of roles around functions*—will require changes in structure in order to re-

spond to the vision of the Council. These include the parish, the diocese, religious orders, missionary congregations, the organizations of the lay apostolate, and so on.

The parish is not treated in any systematic way by the Council documents. It is mentioned about ten times, and although mention is made of a parish council, no concrete guidelines are given for establishing one.

In fact the Council gave very little concrete direction in terms of the restructuring of any of these institutions, and because of this we are now in a period of search, trial, and experimentation. We are also in a period of immobility on the part of some members of these institutions as a result of differences in the views taken of the aims of the Council and also of a previous formation which was too legalistic.

Institutional changes have been made by the Council, but again these primarily concern the bishops. The affirmation of collegiality, the national episcopal conferences, and the Synod of bishops are examples of change at the hierarchical level.

Mixed reactions have greeted the establishment of the Church's new structure, the Synod of bishops, and of course only time will prove whether this body can be an effective means for the exercise of the collegial function of the bishops. The great weakness in the present structure is that it will not function automatically, but will be called into session at the discretion of the Pope to discuss an agenda already prepared. The hope had been to have a permanent senate, composed of representatives of the national conferences of bishops, meeting at regular intervals of once or twice a year to discuss questions proposed by members of the senate.

But we should not be entirely pessimistic about the present arangement, because Pope Paul left the way open for changes in the structure by admitting that "like all human institutions [the Synod] can be still more perfected with the passage of time." And there are many ways of bringing questions which should be placed on the agenda to the atention of the Pope.

At the beginning of this book we said that the changes we are now facing are the result of the transformation in the situation of man in the world through technology and in the Church as a result of the Council. Each institution of the Church has to be examined in the light of this double movement. Let us take, as a concrete example, the parish.

One of the major changes in the life of man as a result of technology has been the development of the city. However, it is only recently that we have become aware of the city as a way of life, as an entity, which will influence the behavior of man in many ways and have a formative effect on his whole set of values. This knowledge is important for the Church because it is something she must take into consideration in terms of her pastoral work as well as of her prophetic mission in society.

The knowledge that a city is more than just an accumulation of neighborhoods and is, in fact, a whole way of life, with a special "form" or "shape" resulting from its functions, will indicate that pastoral planning must be in terms of the whole city. We can no longer think of pastoral care just in terms of the parish. For some time the only form of pastoral care in the city was the parish, and it is still often thought of primarily as a natural community where the pastor should know all the people and should provide for all their religious needs. The concept of pastoral care as a city-wide responsibility is only gradually becoming a reality.

What is the role of the parish in the post-conciliar Church?

The parish is still very important because it is the *center for worship.* The parish church should be a place of worship for everyone of all races, ages, and social conditions; it should be an expression of the universality of the Church. The parish should not be thought of as a natural community; it is, rather, the place where the Eucharistic community is actualized.

In an urban society the liturgy has more and more importance in building up the consciousness of Christian community because in a city and in a mobile world there is less sociological support for a natural community. It is through the liturgy that the Kingdom of God is already present on earth, and all the people at its celebration must really and very consciously form a community, so that any person coming there will feel a part of this

Eucharistic community whether he has ever seen any of these people before or will ever see any of them again.

But the actualization of the Eucharistic community is not for the purpose of withdrawing from the world to spend an hour together: it is to have a reference to life. This reference to life is brought to the consciousness of people through the homily. The celebration of the Mass is not a parenthesis in our lives, somewhere we come to forget our lives. But we come as we are, we offer our whole life as it is, and we must express in some way the fact that this celebration is continued in our lives in order to help us become what we are called to become: witnesses to Christ in the world.

There can be no profound and meaningful liturgical renewal if this is not related to the meaning of the Christian in the world. And we cannot have a real presence of Christians in the world if they are not conscious of the centrality of the Eucharist in their lives.

The primary function of the parish, then, is the actualization of the Eucharistic community. But what can we say about this community as a *human* community, and not only a supernatural community? What are its requisites from a psychological and sociological point of view?

Sociologists speak of three main social forms: *category, group,* and *aggregate.* The term *category* is used to designate people having similar characteristics—for example, "women," "teen-agers," "pre-schoolers." This is just a logical concept, a statistical unit; it does not represent any actual grouping in society. One can speak of "church-going people" as a category, and this can be studied sociologically: age, education, sex, etc. But the people in church on Sunday morning who are forming the Eucharistic community are real people, actually there, and not just a logical concept.

The second concept of social form is the *group.* This is used to refer to people gathered together who have a common goal, which may be weakly expressed but which exists, some kind of interpersonal relationship, and some kind of organization. For example, "workers" could be called a "category," but as soon as they become conscious of their similiarities and begin to organize, they form a "group."

When we look at the Sunday Mass we must conclude that this is not a group. There is a common goal, but the other requisites for a group do not always exist. In a city there is not usually an interrelationship of the people participating in the Mass, and there is no formal or informal organization, except for the fact of being there. So the social form required for the Eucharistic community is not the group.

The third social form is called an *aggregate,* and this is a gathering of people. There are many types of aggregates. If an accident happens on the street, immediately there is an aggregate of people. Another kind of aggregate involves a more social relationship, for example, at lectures, meetings, movies. There is a kind of public participation, maybe very passive, but a type of collective behavior.

The liturgy involves a special type of aggregate which demands more than a passive or merely reactive type of participation. It requires that the people gathered together do something together. The social form of the Eucharistic community (required on a human level) is an *aggregate* form, calling for the *participation* of people gathered together for a specific, well-known purpose, but not involving an interrelationship which demands a formal continuity.

In addition to the people with whom and for whom the liturgical celebration takes place, there are some other social requisites for the Eucharistic assembly.

First, there must be a *place* because this is a gathering of people. There must be some physical location, not necessarily a church, because this gathering can be held in the open air, or in a home, or a hotel room. It is not necessary to have a geographical territory with certain boundaries for the parish liturgy, but just a place where the priest and people can actualize the Eucharistic assembly. Normally, however, a building will be necessary to assure the weekly repetition of the celebration and for other ritual or sacramental actions, a building which will be a visible sign of the purpose for which it exists and will be open and available to anyone who wishes to come there, whether he is a "member" of the parish or not.

A *public* place is needed, an *open* place for the Eucharistic assembly. It would not be normal for the Eucharistic celebration ordinarily to take place for only one specific category of people and not be open to all others. The Eucharistic community must reflect as far as possible the universality of the Church, open to all men, witnessing that all people in the world are invited to this assembly.

I do not say that Mass should not be celebrated for small groups. This can be a very good thing. But it should be just occasionally, and not on a regular, permanent basis. Nor should it be considered as the ideal, because the impression conveyed could be that of limiting the Eucharistic community to the natural community. The only ideal situation of true worship of God will be in the Kingdom of God, where we will all be together without the differences which now divide us. But our Eucharistic celebrations, however imperfect, must be a sign of this ideal situation, and they can only be this if they are ordinarily open to everyone.

Because of the weekly repetition of the celebration, there eventually arises the necessity for some kind of *institution* established on a permanent basis, and with someone to take care of it. As soon as there is an institution, there will be *roles*. Some of these will be permanent, to assure the basic organization, and some will be partial.

A certain *nucleus of people* will generally exist. Supernaturally speaking, the Eucharistic assembly could take place without this, but it will succeed from a human standpoint only if there are people who care about the success of the participation: lectors, leaders of song, accompanying musicians, and so on. The priest and these people, knowing each other and working together, will form a group. This should not be regarded as a closed group or an exclusive group. It should always be open to new members. This group should never identify itself with the Eucharistic community, however, or use the Eucharistic assembly just to make a natural community.

I am not saying anything against interpersonal relationships, or saying that it is desirable for the Eucharistic assembly to be an impersonal assembly. Of course at every Mass there will be some people who know one another, and their bonds of friendship should be deepened and strengthened through the Mass. But the Mass is intended to strengthen the bonds of love among all men, whether they are our close personal friends or not. And we cannot become close personal friends with everyone we meet, however much we might wish to do so.

Worship at the level of the "congregation" is especially important because it offers us a first dimension of universality. And if the Church is to be the sign of close union with God and of the unity of all mankind we must experience some dimension of this union. This does not at all exclude the possibility of instituting in the Church a liturgy for small groups where interpersonal relationship is possible, however. As a matter of fact, such a liturgy should exist if we want to experience meaningfully other dimensions of the Eucharistic assembly—that the Mass is also a meal, for example. But this will require a specific social form, usually a group within a certain category, and efforts to bring characteristics of this type of experience to the level of the congregation will be illusory.

We have somehow identified "Christian" relationship with "primary" relationship, as if it were impossible really to experience a Christian love for people unless we know everything about them and are on terms of continuing relations with them. This is a holdover from the rural, pretechnical civilization when Christian relationship was established within a small, stable community and such a personal relationship was common. But it is no less possible today to carry out more "secondary" relationships in in spirit of Christian love, without trying to make every relationship a "primary" one. A bus driver, for example, can almost ruin one's day or make it much more enjoyable simply by his manner towards his passengers as they enter or leave his bus. Or a sales clerk can regain a sense of humanity when she is thanked for her services with a smile that is given to a person, and not to a service. Secondary relationships carried out in a Christian manner will involve a genuine respect and recognition of the personhood of the other.

But we should not expect every Mass to evolve somehow into a *group* relationship where everyone knows everyone else on a first-name basis, or think that this is

the ideal to be attained. Every Mass should be an experience of Christian community, however, strengthening
the bonds of love which join all men together as brothers
in Christ.

A final consideration for the actualization of the Eucharistic assembly is the *physical disposition* of the
church and of the faithful. The atmosphere of the church
should not be theatrical or artificial or sentimental, but
natural, dignified, and in accordance with the culture.
The celebrant, facing the people, should be visible to
them even when he is sitting. Provision must be made
so that everyone can hear, and this will include some
arrangements to block out exterior noise.

The parish does not have a monopoly on worship, but
this is its fundamental function; to fulfill this a territory
is not essential. There are two other functions of the
parish, however, an *administrative* function and a *specialized* function.

Because we are living in a society where mobility is a
factor in everyday life and social control is much more
diffused, there is a necessity for some records, for some
statistics, and for some division of certain pastoral responsibilities. So the territory of a diocese is divided up
into manageable proportions in order to facilitate this
task. But it should be remembered that the territory is
not the basis for the Eucharistic community. Fidelity to
the Church should not be equated with fidelity to certain
geographical boundaries. The territory is useful for ad-

ministrative functions and for a certain division of work, especially for catechetical work. However, more and more we should assure the liberty of choice in a city for worship and for other religious activities. The administrative aspect of keeping records and the elaboration of statistics may easily be assured by a communication of data to one central ecclesiastical administration or to decentralized geographical units.

In a city it is impossible for one parish to be completely in charge of all pastoral functions. Its pastoral activity will vary according to the place where it is located.

One parish in Paris, for example, is near a railroad station. It has very little territory. It is based on commuters, and there are priests present all the time to hear confessions and for counseling. Specialized meetings are organized during noontime and after work hours, before people leave for home. One of the reasons people stop there is that they can be anonymous. Their lives are lived elsewhere, and they can more openly discuss their problems with priests whom they do not have to see every week. This has become a very active parish.

A parish located in a slum area of the inner city will be called upon for much more social action in its pastoral care. A day care center may be needed, for example, or a job opportunities clinic, or some kind of recreation center.

In the suburbs pastoral care will be directed more to families, and to the aged and sick. Parishes located in university towns will need to offer a different type of pastoral care than parishes located in industrial centers.

All of these specialized functions need to be integrated within a diocese or a pastoral zone, so that the type of pastoral care is supplied where it is most needed. If this is done, the Church may more convincingly witness to the concern of Christ for all his people and their needs.

Social change in roles and in institutions is leading to new definitions and new interpretations. None of these developing suggestions will provide a permanent answer, nor should a permanent answer be sought. It is an ever changing and ever challenging mission to bring the message of the Gospel to all men. But if the Church remains open to the signs of the times, new opportunities will always reveal themselves as they are needed, because the "institutional" Church is a service of the living Church in the world.

RELATIONS WITH OUTSIDE GROUPS

We have said before that the definition of the Church changed the way we are envisaging the other Christian churches. We can no longer say that they are the "out-group," and this is a profound sociological and theological transformation, one which will develop in future types of relationships with other Christians.

But we may still speak of an "outgroup," with new

connotations of course, to indicate the other religious groups and the atheist. The redefinition of the Church and her aims, however, has also had an effect upon the way we perceive our relationship with the other religions and with the atheists.

In 1964 Pope Paul constituted a secretariat for non-believers, and in his encyclical *Ecclesiam Suam* stressed the willingness of the Church to conduct a dialogue with atheists and other non-believers. This marked a real change in our previous attitude, which had alternated between a paternalistic "They are poor, benighted souls" and an aggressive "It is not possible for anyone in good faith to be an atheist!" We are now prepared to accept the fact that an atheism can exist which is non-aggressive in that it does not seek to destroy organized religion, and one which is in many ways open to revelation. The previous image of the Church as having no concern with the problems of this life was certainly a factor in promoting the development of atheism. The negativism of the Church toward human progress had resulted in an image of a God who was almost "jealous" of man's progress, and the efforts of many humanists were directed not so much toward fighting the idea of God as toward promoting the dignity of man.

The new awareness of the Church that the building up of the world is a Christian concern as well as the concern of all men is reason enough for an appeal to all peoples, even Communists, to work together to solve the problems of the world. This change in attitude may hardly seem worth mentioning, since so few results are evident as yet, but it represents a real transformation.

During all the discussions on the Church in the Modern World some bishops were repeatedly calling for the Council to issue a summation of all the errors of the modern world, but especially of Communism. This kept up during the discussion of Schema 13 (The Church in the Modern World) till finally Archbishop Wojtyla of Cracow (now a cardinal) made a very strong plea that Communism should not be condemned. "This document," he said, "is a *dialogue,* and we cannot begin a dialogue by condemning the people we want to talk to. And furthermore, those of us who live in Communist countries are beginning to see some self-questioning among the Marxist intellectuals. If we condemn them, they won't even open the document; if we don't, maybe they will read it and see what the Church has to say about the great problems of the world. We may find we can work together in more ways than we now think."

No dialogue can exist between doctrines, only people can engage in dialogue. And making the distinction between doctrine and people is the necessary first step to dialogue.

Of course the willingness on the part of the Church to engage in dialogue with representatives of other religions and with atheists is a recognition that we have much to learn from a dialogue with others as well as much to give.

This attitude can produce quite a shock among some Catholics who have always thought in terms of the Church *against* the rest of the world. There is a real fear of loss of identity because it is much easier for self-identification to stress differences, to react against another group. This is why some Catholics have reacted so strongly against the relaxing of the Friday abstinence. They fear that "we are becoming just like Protestants!"

These changes in the way the Church has perceived her identity—as the people of God on pilgrimage, participating responsibly in the life of the Church and in the life of the world, open to the world and to all peoples, as the servant of mankind and as the sign of Christ in the world—will necessitate changes in internal structures and in external appearances in order to be faithful to the renewed understanding of the mission of the Church to modern man.

As I said before, if we took a survey today in order to arrive at a definition of the Church and based this definition upon the image of the Church as she appears to men in the world, I do not think our definition would match the one given by the Council. Beneath all the accumulated irrelevancies of twenty centuries of institutional living, I am sure we would be able to discover the message of the Gospel intact, and to find also that our understanding of it had grown and developed over the centuries together with our understanding of man. But in her institutional life, weighted as she is with so much trivia of time, is the Church today really witnessing to the Gospel?

This present-day witness was the concern of Pope John in calling the Council. He was not in doubt of the message of the Gospel, ever new and ever needed, but about the *manner* in which the Church was making this message known to men. We have been told by all the Council documents, in no uncertain terms, to change our style and have been left in no doubt as to what that style is to be. The values of participation, responsibility, freedom, tolerance, service and dialogue are all parts of that style. But these are all values that must be internalized—they cannot be commanded or imposed. And until these values are accepted in the lives of all those responsible for the witness of the Church—that is, in the lives of all Christians—we will experience a period of confusion, anxiety, frustration, and tension.

3 THE SHAKE-UP OF INTERNAL FUNCTIONS

The Church is an institution. Some reject this fact as somehow unworthy of the Kingdom of God existing in mystery on earth till the fullness of time, and would prefer a more mystical and "uncontaminated" mode of existence. And it is easy to share their desire somehow to be free of all the depressing and discouraging examples from past and present history that witness more to human folly and intransigence than to God's message of love and salvation. However, it must be faced that this desire has more in common with Platonic philosophy than it has with the doctrine of the Incarnation.

This is one of the great mysteries of the Church, that she is established in mankind and is to that extent subject to the laws of human nature. And God did not call us simply to an individual faith, but to an assembly, a people. If we are to be a people, visibly witnessing to God's message of salvation in Christ, we must, of human necessity, have some institutional structure in order to maintain an identity.

I make no excuses for the abuses of the institution; that is why the Church constantly needs reform, because she does exist in mankind and is subject to human weakness. But the Church as organization will exist together with the Church as the people of God, both being aspects of the same Church, sacrament of the union with God and of the unity of all mankind.

So the Church shares in common with other social institutions certain *mechanisms* which are necessary for the functioning of the institution: *norms, authority, socialization, communication.*

THE SYSTEM OF NORMS

In each institution there is a certain system of norms which gives that institution its specificity and without which the institution does not exist. In the Church the basic norm upon which the whole institution rests is the *Gospel*, the great orientation given by Christ to his Church. It is the norm of reference for the whole action of the Church and for her organization. Each time the Church has become too much integrated into a culture or a social system, the only way of reforming her was to go back to the Gospel. That is why all kinds of revivals and reforms are also based on a return to the Gospel, to the Bible—at least intentionally, in the minds of the people behind them.

The organization is always secondary and related to the existence of the Church as the People of God, however. It is not an aim in itself either on the universal or on the local level. For example, the *aim* of the Church is not to create parishes. Parishes are a *means* in the pastoral life of the Church to bring people together into a Eucharistic assembly. All the secondary institutions in the Church, and the Church herself as an institution, are *means* for building up the people of God among the children of God.

The *aims* of the Church are essentially dynamic because it is always a new mission to make of all the children of God the people of God. It is always a new challenge because we are living in a very rapidly changing world. But the institution always has a tendency to be static, stable, conservative. So there will always be some tension in the Church as an institution whose aims are essentially dynamic.

Sometimes the tension becomes so great that there is an actual *conflict* between the aims of the Church and the institution as it is. When this happens it is the institution which must be changed. We must always be able to see that the aim of the Church is not to build up or to maintain a particular form of institution, but to bring people into a relationship to God through the concrete mediation of the Church, the manner of this mediation having to change and to be adapted to the times.

What is to be changed? Surely not the Gospel itself, because the Gospel is the basic norm. Our understanding of the Gospel, however, is subject to growth and development, and through the changing situations of mankind a fresh approach may be taken to revelation, resulting in new insights in the ever living encounter between God and man which the Church is.

But there are other norms in the Church, which have developed with the passage of time and have become more or less necessary as the Church has grown in size and complexity. Designed to give answers with regard to the conduct proper under various circumstances, these norms are codified in canon law, in the constitutions of religious congregations, and so on. They are concerned with ecclesiastical authority, the clergy, all the different ecclesiastical institutions, marriage, and many other areas of behavior.

All norms are standards or indications of behavior for a person who is a member of a particular group and are indispensable, to a certain degree, for the group if it is to function as a group. Of course for a small group the norms do not have to be codified, but norms nevertheless exist which are very clear to the members of the group. If a member does not live up to these norms, he is no longer regarded as a member of the group.

The great difficulty, of course, is that as soon as something is actually codified, it is almost "sacralized," especially in minds formed in a legalistic tradition. In the Latin countries such a mentality is quite common. But there is a counterpart to this mentality: it is possible to have a very highly codified set of norms because (in some of the Latin countries, at least) a norm is not something you are supposed to follow, but a goal towards which you are expected to tend. But when a highly codified set of norms is carried to other countries where the law is the law, the interpretation is quite different. That's why it was said that in the Church the Italians were making the laws and the Irish and the Americans were keeping them!

So there are different mentalities which are brought to bear on the meaning of *norms*. The Orientals, too, interpret norms in their own way. I had a conversation with Patriarch Maximos after one of his talks at the Council. He was reacting very strongly to the idea that not saying the breviary, or not attending Mass on Sunday, or eating meat on Friday should be thought of as a "mortal" sin. He said, "In the Orient we don't know what a 'scruple' is. That is a typically Western disease. All this 'mortal' and 'venial' sin comes from your legalistic approach to these matters!" Another Oriental prelate in the Council said one day: "Christ gave his message to the world. We Orientals have made a *mystique* out of it—but you Occidentals, you have made a code of canon law!"

The understanding of codified norms, then, is different according to different cultures. We have been accustomed to only one approach, a quite legalistic one, which enforced a very exacting manner of behavior in some countries and was practically ignored in others, according to the cultural environment. At the present time this codified set of norms is in real conflict, in many instances, with what is happening in the Church. Our relations with other Christians, for example, come immediately to mind. Canon law is completely out-of-date in this area.

The fact that not only in the world, where wholly new problems are arising, but in the Church itself the acceleration of change has been tremendous has had many effects on the whole system of norms, beginning with the definition of the Church and all the norms related to this. Changes in canon law will be necessary to meet the orientation of the Council. There is no need to detail all these changes here; almost every decree of the Council calls for a rethinking of some part of canon law. In some cases a complete suppression of the present law is called for. New guidelines are needed for the organization of new structures in the Church, especially in regard to the Synod of bishops, the national episcopal conferences, the priests' senates, the participation of the laity, and so on.

The commission on the revision of canon law set up by Pope John did not work during the Council; it had to wait for the Council documents. It has been at work since the Council, however, and has had a great deal to accomplish.

The revision of canon law will be a real test of the

success or failure of the Council, not so much in terms of concrete decisions as in the whole philosophy which underlies the revision. The legalistic, juridical approach must give way to a more flexible approach, with an awareness of personal responsibility of the mature conscience, with a respect for the dignity and rights of all persons, and with a sense of the necessity for "institutionalizing change" if the reform is to be meaningful.

The situation of transition is not a very comfortable one because on one side there is the Council with all its forward movement and on the other the former code. While this code is still the norm it would seem to call for continued observance, although when it is in direct conflict with the mind of the Council I do not see how it can exert much binding force on the conscience. It can be observed, of course, as a way of keeping cohesion in the group.

The present condition of the Church is best described, perhaps, as a certain state of *anomie*. This is a term used to describe the predicament of a group in the process of change and no longer certain of its norms. A state of *anomie* is very typical, for example, among immigrants. For some time they do not know which norms to observe: those of the old country or those of the new. The same thing is true, also, of Negroes coming from the rural South to live and work in the industrial North, and this condition can be prolonged for more than one generation if the people are forced to live in a ghetto. It is to the

benefit of everyone concerned if the process of integration
can progress more normally, because this state of *anomie*
is extremely difficult and should not be prolonged. We see
the same condition in young people all over the world
who refuse to adopt the values of adult society but have
not yet agreed on their own set of values. Societies which
undergo rapid urbanization or rapid industrialization
without a period of time to acquire the cultural values
which normally accompany this process also find themselves in a state of *anomie*.

So in a certain way, this is the present state of the
Church. It is a difficult period and, as I said, should not
be unnecessarily prolonged. But we must avoid the temptation to make a new codex of canon law in a hurry just
to "fix" the situation, to organize the results of the Council so that we know exactly what everyone should do,
and then "freeze" everything till the next revision.

The great problem for the Church as an institution in
the modern world is to assure enough general norms to
maintain unity and self-identification, but also to be sure
that the possibility for change and diversity is *permanently incorporated* into the structure, so that when a
need for change arises the existing norms do not have to
be *broken*. Before the Council this was almost the only
way to change the norm. About the only mechanism was
to have a sufficient number of what I would call "prophetic personalities" openly breaking the "law." This was
true in the liturgy, in parish work, in the lay apostolate,

in more collective approaches to pastoral work, and in other areas. We see a similar situation today in the areas of birth control and priestly celibacy, and it is unfortunate that these issues were not permitted to be discussed in the Council. The process of changing law by breaking it leads to cynicism, and it is certainly not normal for it to be the only course available in an institution composed of rational beings. So we must include in our norms the possibility of change and some mechanisms which will allow us to institutionalize change.

One of the temptations of the authority in an institution, in a situation of *anomie* and in a period of rapid change, is to insist on the absolute value of norms in order to prevent laxity, and to impose those norms as the objects of obedience. This approach is prompted by fear, and it is an ineffective way of reacting, because there are now very few people who will accept such treatment. Instead it adds to the danger of the situation by creating a "credibility gap."

In fact it is because we have given such an "absolute" value to almost all norms established by the institutional Church that we are experiencing so much difficulty now. Our whole Western Christian culture became oriented to the almost absolute and binding character of the law, and in order to implement the law, the impression was given that almost all norms were absolute. For example, just a few years ago it was considered a mortal sin to have a drink of water during the Eucharistic fast and—remem-

bering that one had done so—then receive communion.
Could we really believe that people who had eaten meat
on Friday were damned for eternity? This was not really
the spirit of canon law, but in our pastoral work some
codified norms were presented as being as important as
those of the Gospel itself. Our catechetics had formed
such a juridical spirit that almost all norms were put on
the same level, and we have the example from the Gree-
ley-Rossi survey on the Catholic schools of those young
people who put Friday abstinence *above* love of neighbor.

Now we must insist upon the provisional character of
most norms. This is something we will have to learn in
the Catholic Church. By stressing that norms have a provisional character, in the sense that they may be changed
with new circumstances, it is possible to continue to observe them temporarily for the good of the group. And
this will even be true, we must realize, of the norms contained in revelation. In fact the provisional character of
most "absolute" prohibitive moral norms has long been
recognized, among them the "exceptions" to the com-
mandments "Thou shalt not kill," "Thou shalt not steal,"
and "Thou shalt not bear false witness." There is a deep
relationship between the basic norm of love of God and
neighbor and the expression of this relationship in norms
of human morality. Our understanding of this relationship grows and changes as our knowledge of man in-
creases. This knowledge must always be taken into ac-

count in all our moral teaching. This will demand a constant attention to the meaning of revelation in the life of man and a new reading of the Gospel in accord with the "signs of the times."

A provisional character must be recognized even more in codified norms imposed by the institutional Church. It is not hard to recognize that some norms are necessary for the cohesion of the group, but it is not necessary to treat them as if they were to endure forever.

The whole question of the priest's wearing a cassock, for example, illustrates how certain cultures can influence the enforcement of canonical norms. In some cultures a priest is obliged to wear his cassock on all occasions. This canonical dress, which is mandatory in Rome but which may be imposed upon clerics elsewhere at the decree of the bishop, became a sign, in the nineteenth century, of the victory of the Church over the French Revolution. It was a sign that the Church could once again hold a recognized position in society, and for a long time in Europe it was considered lamentable that priests in the United States, Great Britain and Germany wore suits. It seemed to be a sign that the Church was not fully accepted in society. And one of the large preoccupations of some bishops in Mexico, till not so long ago, was the day when priests would be permitted to wear the cassock on the street again, because that would be a sign that the revolution was over!

And at the same time there are priests thinking that

they should dress the same as everyone else in the society in which they are living to avoid the possibility of social prestige or special treatment. But in any case, where the norm means different things in different societies, it will be easier to observe if it is not made an "absolute."

The present structure of the Mass, for example, could be improved. But knowing that improvement will come, it is possible to maintain the present structure without too much impatience and to work creatively within it. Or a priest will find it more possible to live with a difficult assignment if he knows that some institutional possibilities are available for adjusting or terminating the assignment.

Many norms are completely outmoded, of course, and we must use common sense in dealing with these. Their observance is a matter of fact as well as a matter of faith, and in each case we must use responsible judgment. In Belgium, for example, before the Council it was a law that a priest could be suspended if he went to the movies. This has been changed now, but priests have been going to movies and saying Mass the next day for years!

All kinds of now ridiculous norms are still in existence, but they have been ignored for some time. Of course it is much better not to have this kind of norm at all, and the revision of canon law could go a long way in seeing that it becomes obsolete. Norms of this kind are completely out of place in a Church of responsible Christian adults.

One of the first works of the Synod will be to examine the new code of canon law, and the outcome of this encounter will be of great importance for the future of the post-conciliar Church.

THE SYSTEM OF AUTHORITY

In any institution there exists not only a system of norms, but also a system of *authority*. If we look at authority from the standpoint of the institution, we see that authority is an exercise of social control. This has nothing to do with the direct control of one person by another. It is a much broader concept and includes *all forms of control exercised to keep the group together as a group.*

Authority exists in a social institution to maintain the cohesion of the group, to coordinate different types of activity, and to exercise some social control. Social control and cohesion of the group are not aims in themselves. But to achieve the purpose of the group there must be a consciousness of unity. The normal function of authority is not to impose cohesion, but to make the group more able to perform the aims for which the group exists.

The possibilities for different types or systems of authority in the Church are very great; the concrete forms of authority were not revealed by Christ. His references to authority were in terms of *service*. In history the forms develop and change according to circumstances. Some have been more democratic than others.

At different times and places bishops have been elected by their fellow bishops, by the canons of the cathedral, or by the people. They have been appointed by the civil authority, nominated by the king or named directly by the pope. In recent years a highly complicated and extremely secret method has been used which leaves much to be desired when held up to the ideals of the Council.

As a whole we may say that because the Church is now envisaged more as the people of God than as an organization, the importance given to the function of authority will decrease. A greater flexibility will exist in the ways the members of the Church will express their belonging to the Church through the multiplicity of their commitments in the world and through various forms of prayer and worship. There is some danger of anarchy, it is true. But a dogmatic exercise of authority will only result in a "marginalization" of the authority, less and less relevant for the more thoughtful Christians.

Collegiality

What the Second Vatican Council has done with the emphasis on the collegiality of the bishops in the governing of the Church is to bring the whole system of authority in the Church from a monarchical type to a more democratic type. Not from monarchy to democracy, but from one type to another. Only a few steps have been taken, but they are important ones.

Collegiality is not simply a new way of exercising authority. It is a theological concept based on the responsibility of the bishops—through their consecration as bishops—to participate with the Pope as head of their "college" in the governing of the universal Church. It is not to be thought of as a juridical right conferred upon them by the Pope.

In a certain way, the rediscovery of the theological concept of collegiality was brought about by the evolution of the modern world. It is an evident fact that all decisions in the Church cannot be made today by the Pope, if indeed they ever could. Today the Church is much too complex, the cultural and geographical spread is too great. We are more aware than ever before that we are living in a complex society in a complex world. The concept of collegiality was reinforced by the systems of modern communication and transportation because the concrete functioning of this concept is now actually possible. So even if the theological definition of collegiality was not intended directly to effect a change in authority in the Church, psychologically and sociologically it has had a very important influence.

One effect is the *Synod of bishops*. After the vote on

collegiality in the third session of the Council, it was almost impossible not to constitute some concrete expression of this theological reality, and Pope Paul announced the news of the Synod at the beginning of the fourth session.

Another result is the formation of *national episcopal conferences*. Some countries already had episcopal conferences, but it was the Council which gave them a new importance and role. Many issues which concern the Church cannot be solved at the level of one diocese because the diocese is no longer a sociological unit. Pastoral policy cannot be confined to one diocese because many problems exist on a national level: education, health, poverty, racial equality, communication. This is true not only of problems in society but also of institutional concerns in the Church, and especially since the Council: the liturgy, the diaconate, ecumenism, the missions, the organizations of the lay apostolate, seminaries, catechetical instruction, and so on.

Therefore, these two structures represent the possibility of a new type of authority, one which gives the bishop a greater role in the governing of the universal Church and lessens his authority somewhat at the local level. They provide a way of decentralizing some of the authority of Rome and of centralizing some of the authority of each country. This two-way process can be of real value to the universality of the Church if a balance can be maintained in the concrete exercise of authority at these levels.

Channels of Information

The functioning of authority in the Church is also related to *information,* and the more complex the institution, the more need there is for information.

One of the problems of the modern world is that there is almost too much information available and the process of selectivity becomes more difficult all the time. How do we know which information is relevant? We need organized and meaningful information, competently evaluated. I don't think pastors can get this only by reading the newspapers and magazines or by visiting people or by keeping an "open door" policy. This type of information will be generally too fragmented to serve as a basis for meaningful action. We must have different channels of information, and these I would divide into two main types: *living information* and *statistics.*

Living information is to be obtained by personal contacts, not just those made at random, but on a more organized basis. This type of organization for information is just evolving in the Church. It includes commissions and councils composed not only of priests, but of lay people and members of religious congregations, and at all levels in the Church: parochial, diocesan, regional, national, and international. The value of these commissions or councils will depend to a great extent upon how well they are set up. Their purpose, in a collegial church, is to get information from the *periphery* to the *center*. They should be set up to form some sort of permanent base for supplying the kind of information that will be useful in determining needed action throughout the Church.

It would not be wise at any of these levels for members of these commissions to be simply appointed by the presiding authority, except at certain levels where professional competence is a matter for concern. For example, it will not be too useful for a pastor simply to choose his board of parishioners for a parish council, because, human nature being what it is, he will probably choose a majority whose opinions will agree with his own.

The Council, apart from proposing the idea that parish councils should be established throughout the diocese, as well as a senate of priests and a pastoral council, did not propose the method for their selection. But the principle of some kind of elected representation should be followed if the result of obtaining wider information is to be achieved.

It might be possible, for example, to elect one or two representatives from each of the areas of activity in the parish to serve on the parish council: the liturgy commission (which would include those serving as lectors, leaders of song, acolytes, choir, etc.); religious education (CCD, school board, teachers, assistants); business and finance committee; social action groups; ecumenical groups, and so on.

This would presuppose, of course, that each parish had

already *involved* its members in these various areas, and though every parish would certainly not duplicate all the organizations of every other parish, some lay involvement in several of these areas should exist if there has been any serious attempt on the part of the pastor to implement the action of the Council. It would produce a meaningless façade for a pastor simply to appoint someone to represent all these areas if, in fact, there was no underlying commitment represented. In cities where combined pastoral action has been organized in some of these areas, representation might be on a city-wide basis. However, more and more the commitment of Christians in the world will not be achieved solely in Christian organizations, and we must find the ways of including people from these broader spheres of activity. Otherwise the specific Christian community will become irrelevant for them and at the same time isolated from "the world."

Diocesan, national, and international representatives could be chosen from the elected members of the preceding structure and from appointees or candidates "at large," and there would probably be some "ex officio" members at the different levels. There may be other and better ways that will become more evident as time and experience instruct us. It would also be helpful to investigate some Protestant structures where the experience of such mechanisms is already very old.

Now if, in all this "structuring," I seem to leave no room for the prophetic voice, one which is not "struc-

tured" in an institution, it is not because I underestimate
its importance in the least. The prophetic role, for example, of the *National Catholic Reporter* in the United
States is important. But there is an even greater need for
the prophetic voice to be raised within the institutional
structure. It is the *whole* Church which must speak *as
the Church* with a prophetic voice, especially in the
world situation today.

And only by giving the widest possible opportunity
for the involvement of all Christians in the life and witness of the Church at all levels will it be possible to give
rise to the prophetic voice of the Church in concert. This
is what happened at the Council. The Church as hierarchy spoke prophetically. But now the Church as the
people of God must act in a prophetic manner, her message must be heard in society. Some have despaired of
the possibility that the institutional Church can ever re-
cover the spirit of prophecy. I do not. It happened at the
Council. It is happening today in many parts of the
Church in the world. But it is the task of all Christians.

The Chicago association of priests, for example, organized before the constitution of a presbyterial council, has
provided a prophetic witness of the Church in that city,
and a witness that is more meaningful because it represents a consensus of a group rather than a single voice.

So all of these developing structures in the Church
offer the opportunity for meaningful implementation of
the Council's stress on the collegial exercises of authority

in the Church. They provide a channel for living information and witness at all levels in the Church and could make possible a profound transformation of the institutional presence of the Church in the world. Because the institution which is the Church is, first of all, the people of God.

The second channel of information in the Church is more technical and systematic: *statistics*. This is related more to the administrative functioning of the Church, but it also contributes to the prophetic mission of the Church in its own undramatic way. Statistics provide a collective form of information based on social and cultural groups. Pope Paul has set up an institute in Rome for religious statistics. The director of an important firm making computers, who is not a Catholic, is an appointed member of the commission, an indication that the institute is to function without a bias.

What are some concrete ways in which statistical data can be useful? Here is one example. A large survey was made in Latin America between 1958 and 1962 by the International Federation of Socio-Religious Research (FERES). In addition to providing much other information, the survey made it possible to make a projection on the number of priests the Church would have in the Latin American countries over the coming years. In order to do this, we had to know the age of every priest in Latin America. The Church at this time was not keeping very good statistics, so it took three years to get this information. The feeling had been that the situation was getting much better in Latin America and that the Church did not have to be too greatly concerned about the shortage of pastoral care in the future. As the survey turned out, the situation until 1970 did seem more encouraging, but we concluded that after that date the Latin American Church could not even hope to keep the same proportion of pastoral care, even with increased outside help. This information was helpful in determining pastoral policy and was, I think, instrumental in gaining acceptance of the idea of the restoration of the diaconate.

It also helped to support other initiatives. In Brazil, for example, sisters are providing almost complete pastoral care in some parishes. They do not say Mass or hear confessions, but they are giving communion, baptizing, witnessing marriages, preaching, teaching, and so on. This is being done on an experimental level, but I think it will become permanent.

Statistics could be useful also in another area: for example, our understanding of vocations. Everyone knows that something is happening. But what is the situation? Just in the United States, for example, are fewer people entering the seminaries and religious congregations? Are more leaving? In what dimension and in what proportion? And why?

Well, before saying *why*, we have to know *what*. What are the facts? Upon what are we basing our conclusions?

Someone will say, for example, that the youth of today is not the same as before. They are bad; they sing all these new songs and dance all these new dances, and what can you expect? Or somebody else will base his diagnosis simply upon the more optimistic or pessimistic orientation of his personality. Or upon a few personal contacts and the type of information he has. Maybe one has information based on two or three seminarians he met this week, or another saw the guardian of the Franciscans in this or that province last week. And so on. All this information might come to some mixture that corresponds to reality, but it is not too likely according to the laws of probability.

We need better statistics in order to provide better pastoral care. At least every ten years the Church needs a census in each diocese. Some other data—baptisms, marriages, Mass attendance on Sunday, funerals, and so on—must be kept annually. Organized statistical work is needed at the central level in the Church as well. It will be necessary to report exact data each year, and this will mean more detailed administrative work, but it is necessary.

The responsible use of statistics is a way of getting a new form of knowledge about the religious behavior in a diversified and pluralistic society, in a technical way and no longer in just a personal way. Each diocese should have someone in charge of statistical information and

permanent centers for evaluation set up in various regions
or on an inter-diocesan level. Persons trained in research
and interpretation are needed in each country. This is
the role of CARA (Center of Applied Research on the
Apostolate) in Washington, D.C., for example.

I know that for many persons "statistics" could almost
serve as a synonym for all that is institutional, sterile,
and de-personalized and that to speak of its need in the
Church seems almost sacrilegious: "The Church has more
need of prophets than of statisticians!" I think we need
both, and as I said before, statistics can contribute to the
prophetic mission of the Church. It is often said that anything can be proved by statistics, and this is true enough
—if you are trying to prove an ideology, rather than to
find the truth. I am concerned with the use of statistics in
the Church only to find whatever truth can be found with
their use. Statisticians can be as unpopular as prophets!
But in the Church their mission is the same: to proclaim
what is in reference to what ought to be. And for an
institution such as the Church we do not need a big
super-administration to do this. A few dedicated men
with the necessary tools are enough.

Statistics are not an end in themselves. They need evaluation and interpretation and are valuable only insofar
as they are a *means* of helping to fulfill the *aims* of the
Church.

All these methods for obtaining information—commissions, priests' councils, pastoral councils, parish coun-

cils, statistics—are for the purpose of greater participation by all the people of God in the life of the Church.

Forms of Social Control

The transformation of the system of authority from a more monarchical to a more democratic type also brings about a transformation in the forms of social control, that is, in the ways of maintaining the cohesion of the group.

The greatly reduced emphasis given to the *Index*, for example, is an indication of this transformation. Its very existence has been resented very much, at least psychologically, outside the Catholic Church, and it has not been too popular inside the Church, either!

The reform of the *Holy Office* is another sign of the transformation. There is, to begin with, a change of name: it is no longer the "Holy Office" but the "Congregation for the Doctrine of the Faith." There is also an announced change in the methods of procedure: from now on no theologian is to have his work condemned or suppressed without being first given a hearing. Normal justice has been functioning like this for some time, but this was not the way of the Holy Office!

The Congregation for the Doctrine of the Faith is to have not only the negative task of "watch dog" but also the positive task of promoting necessary theological study in the Church. This new method of procedure may require some time to take hold—I know of no "instant reformation"—but it has been constituted.

The Curia

In modern society there exists, in the whole system of authority, a phenomenon described by sociologists as *bureaucracy*. Bureaucracy is a factor in the life of the Church as well. The bureaucracy of the Church at the central level is called the *Curia*.

Most bishops in the Church were not aware of the power of the Roman Curia, and it took two sessions of the Council for many of them to discover the methods the Curia was using to try to keep control.

To understand how the Curia achieved such a position of influence, it is necessary to go into the history of its development. This will be just a rapid analysis.

The Council of Trent was a reaction to the division of the Church and was very much concerned with the problem of maintaining unity. The accent was placed on external methods and signs of unity: the Latin language in the liturgy, seminary training of priests, canon law, the Index. These tended to a greater centralization of power and decision in Rome. The decadence in the Church at this time was great, and many reforms were needed. To accomplish these reforms, methods of strict control and highly centralized power in the Church were employed.

This process continued for three and a half centuries with ever increasing centralization until the next Council: the First Vatican.

Vatican Council I treated only the primacy of the Pope and did not change the administrative organization of the Church. But the doctrinal affirmation of the primacy of the Pope changed the *spirit* of the organization very much by strongly reinforcing the centralization.

The first reform of the Curia began with Pope Pius X when he reduced the number of Congregations from thirty to eleven. But this reform resulted in even more centralization of power in the Curia.

Under Pope Pius XII the centralization reached its apogee. (Pius XII was his own Secretary of State.) The whole spirit of the Curia became almost psychologically identified with the primacy of the Pope. This was reinforced by the Canon Law of 1918, which had stated that the "Holy See" means the whole Curia. So little by little these events have contributed to an assumption of power by an administrative organization.

It is not hard to understand, from a sociological standpoint, why this transfer of power took place if we take two reference points in history: Vatican I and Vatican II, with almost one hundred years in between. In 1869, there were about 600 bishops, and in 1962 almost 3,000. A direct contact between all the bishops and the Pope was no longer possible. And the whole situation of the Church had been greatly complicated by the population increase and the increase in the complexity of modern civilization during the last century, not only in the "mission" countries of Asia and Africa, but also in the traditionally Christian countries of the Western world. The Pope alone could not possibly exercise authority over this whole complex presence of the Church.

So because the Church is a *living* social body a social adaptation took place. In a living body, when one organ cannot exercise its proper function, another organ takes over this function in a compensatory way. The authority in the Church could not function in the person of one man, so it was sociologically normal for this authority to be exercised by another body—and this was the Curia. From the sociological point of view it was a very healthy phenomenon, but not from the point of view of sound theology in the Church.

When a document came out, then, which said: "The Holy See says that or thinks this" the question was: what *was* the Holy See? Was it the Pope? In most cases not. It might be the thirteenth secretary of the eleventh Congregation! This was one of the things the Council taught the bishops: the relative value of a document coming from the Holy See.

In order to maintain obedience to authority, an emphasis was put on the "sacredness" of the Curia and this had the normal effect on the psychology of its members. Very honestly they came to identify their thinking with the mind of the Church, and to establish an identification between the "Holy See" and the "Church," or between the "Curia" and the "Church." Anyone who dared to disagree with them was disagreeing with the Church. And this was even worse, because the members of the Curia were very devoted to the ecclesiastical institution and to this conception of the Church.

This was perhaps one of the reasons for the Council: Pope John may have decided he couldn't reform the Curia without the help of all the bishops of the Church. And when he announced the Council, the consternation in Rome was great: the Church had just about reached perfection in her organization!

The evaluation of the Curia as a sociological phenomenon is also explained in part by its method of recruitment. Members of the Curia were almost all Italian. The question of Italian nationality is not the point; the situation would not have been much different if they had all been Irish or French. The point is that they were almost all recruited from the same cultural milieu. Many of them achieved positions through personal influence, by knowing the "right" person. And according to the position of one's "protector," one's chances were better or worse.

Attempts were made to internationalize the Curia, but these failed. Either the new men did not fit in and left, or they became absorbed by the group and adopted the same values. As long as there was recruitment from one cultural background this could not be avoided, since the whole set of values was usually held in common and often quite special to the group. There were some advantages to such a system, especially for the cohesion of the administrative body, but the value of universality suffered.

There was also a very exalted view of the mission of the Curia on the part of its members. This is almost always true of a bureaucracy, but it is especially so when it is a "sacred" administration. They really felt they were holding the Church together.

These men were very good priests, and many of them worked hard in outside pastoral positions. It was not so much the problem of the person as it was a social problem. Part of it was, for example, the *career*, with all its values of prestige and protocol. Members of the Curia were just living in another world, and this was the result not so much of a personal attitude as of a sociological development. The Curia had become a social entity in itself, with its own culture, and had assumed more and more authority in the Church. And for a time this was a necessary thing.

But once we realize that the development of the Curia was *sociologically normal* we are able to recognize why its position of authority is *theologically abnormal*, because the Church was not founded by Christ to be governed by the Pope and the Curia, and surely not by the Curia and the Pope, but by the *Pope and the bishops*.

It was this theological teaching which was rediscovered by the Council, as was the whole emphasis put upon authority as a *service*. This transformation in the concept of authority in the Church is quite profound. It is the work of the post-conciliar Church to bring this concept to life.

The process of reforming the Curia is not an easy one. Pope Paul took three steps before performing a major revision. First he made a few of the most necessary changes in the Curia itself, in line with the strongest criticism of the Curia made at the Council—for example, the reform of the Holy Office. Then he developed what could be called a "parallel curia" with new organisms to respond to the new needs. About ten secretariats and permanent commissions were constituted: Secretariats for Unity, for Non-Believers, a Pontifical Commission for Justice and Peace, and so on. Finally he appointed a few non-Italian Curia members.

The major step came in the middle of 1967, with quite a few innovations: a temporary period of appointment; a greater responsibility of residential bishops in the central organs; a policy of appointing non-Italians; an administrative reorganization: finances, statistics, etc. All this is going in the right direction: institutionalization of change, new relations between the periphery and the center, new channels of information.

But two major questions remain. By whom will this reform be implemented? And will the flexibility of the new organisms like the Secretariat for Unity or the Commission for Justice and Peace be respected in the new organization? In other words, a change in organization, even if positive, has meaning only if it is at the service of values, and in this case, at the service of the values not only expressed, but in a certain way "liberated," by the Council.

THE SOCIALIZATION PROCESS

The mechanism used by an institution to make an individual a member of the group is called a process of *socialization.* It is the process used to introduce the member to the beliefs, norms, and behavior of the group. In some institutions this is a long-term process, in others a rapid one, but it is essentially one of *education.*

The mechanism through which the Church exercises the function of education in Christian values is called *catechetics.* This is much more than just an intellectual process; it is an introduction to the faith and a transmission of fundamental religious values. The goal is not knowledge alone but practice. This whole sector is of primary importance because it corresponds to the whole internal aim of the Church.

In the history of the Church there have been times and places where the whole culture was formed by the Church, where everyone had the faith, and it was assumed that in this Christian society where all shared the same values, the natural means of family and social environment were enough to assure the transmission of religious values. Very little effort beyond the Sunday sermon was devoted by the Church to provide a systematic process of socialization.

For many sociological reasons—the development of a pluralistic society following the Protestant revolt, changes in family life, new emphasis on education, and so on— a more highly organized system of socialization was developed by the Church. Various catechisms were written and compiled, the Confraternity of Christian Doctrine was founded in 1560 and approved by Pope Pius V in 1571, the training of catechists was provided for by the Council of Trent, and the retreat movement developed. All are examples of organized methods of socialization in the Church.

However, the greater part of catechetical work in the Church since the Reformation has been devoted to children and has developed over the years into an extensive Catholic school system which undertakes to provide not only catechetical instruction but secular instruction in all subjects as well. This system became so extensive that canon law makes attendance at Catholic schools mandatory.

The history of the development of the Catholic school system is a study in itself, but it will be useful to review just a few important points. The first schools established and administered by religious congregations of men and women were for the poor. Secular subjects were taught and instructions in religion were also given. In a society where the value of education was growing, where knowing how to read and write was becoming more and more necessary, the action of the Church in providing this schooling was a real service to society.

The cultural evolution of Western society was such that more education began to be required in all subjects and, because of the development of a technological culture, more specialized and highly technical advanced training was needed. The grade school education that was once quite adequate became only the first step in a process that is becoming more and more involved. Today in many fields even a college degree is only the beginning.

So education has become a recognized value in our society, to the extent that attendance at school until a certain age is required by law in many States. Today there are more young people going to school, and they are staying in school for many more years than formerly. This situation, of course, necessitates a tremendous financial investment, and the cost of education represents a significant proportion of the taxes collected by the civil government. In some countries the Catholic schools are supported by the State, but in many others they receive little if any State financial support, and it is becoming impossible for the Catholic schools to continue to match the quality of education offered by the public schools.

The Church has made a significant contribution to society in helping to secure the recognition of education as a basic human right, and for the peoples in the developing countries of Latin America, Africa and Asia she still has a role to play in helping to obtain and secure this right. But in the developed countries of the Western world, it has been obtained and recognized, and the State is providing education. In these countries Catholic education is no longer a service to society, but rather a specific service to the Catholic group, and to society only indirectly. It can be useful to Catholics, but it can also produce a climate of competition with the public schools or a complete loss of interest in the public school system.

The Church must continue, of course, to be concerned about the religious education and formation of her members, but the continued maintenance and further expansion of an extensive system of Catholic schools is not the only way to perform this function, nor is it necessarily the best way in today's society. The Catholic school system is, at best, providing for an ever diminishing proportion of Catholic young people, because there are more children to educate than there are schools available.

The North American Church cannot possibly continue indefinitely to finance the building of more new Catholic schools to meet the needs of an increasing school population, and it is at present providing schools for less than half the children of elementary school age. At the high school level the cost is becoming so great that although all the parishes must contribute to the support of central high schools, it is often only the children of well-to-do parents who can afford to attend them. So the service that is provided at this level is even narrower. This is a very common situation in various European countries as well, such as Belgium and France, in Latin America and to a certain extent also in Asia and Africa.

At all levels it is becoming more and more difficult to staff and maintain the schools we now have. The number of priests and sisters available to teach in them is steadily declining, and qualified lay people teaching in Catholic schools are demanding, and quite justly, higher salaries.

Increasing numbers of Catholics are attending the public schools from the elementary level through the university, and recent studies have shown that the religious quality of young people is influenced more by the values found in the home than by the training given in the Catholic school; it is a positive complement to the influence of the family.

All these factors, then, seem to demand that we take a new look at our present commitment to the Catholic school system as the main expression of the function of socialization in the Church.

Parishes and dioceses must go so deeply into debt to maintain this system that they are obliged to neglect many other efforts. We are sometimes forced to place such an emphasis on the financial support of the Church to pay for and maintain a vast complex of educational institutions that it is little wonder that the witness of the Church is obscured.

It would be very illuminating to conduct an extensive and comprehensive survey to find out just how much money is absorbed yearly by the Catholic school system and what percentage of the Catholic population this financial outlay serves, then compare this figure with the amount spent on programs for the poor, for those in the inner city, for research, for aid to the developing countries, for CCD programs, for Newman centers, for marriage preparation, and the like. The internalization of values and norms in each member of the Church—and this is what catechetics is all about—is a permanent and continuing aim of the Church. The Church must provide pastoral care for *all* her members, adults as well as children, all students in the public schools as well as those in Catholic schools. But as long as the present situation continues, we cannot finance creative and necessary experiments designed to reach all the people and not just the select few. No money is available for centers of research, day-care centers in the inner city, social centers for young people, friendship houses, "half-way" houses, centers of religious education for adults and young adults with the latest and the best in books, movies, lectures, filmstrips, and the best people to staff these centers.

The Church is not a social welfare agency, of course, but she does live her life in society, and it is in society, and not just in the privacy of her "own" institutions, that she is to witness to Christ.

In discussing the possibility of gradually disengaging

the Catholic Church from maintaining a complete and separate school system, and of replacing this form of socialization in Christian values with other approaches, there is one practical problem that is raised repeatedly: the public schools are taking over so much of the social as well as the academic education of their students with all sorts of after-school activities—athletics, band and glee-club concerts, school clubs, dances, and so on—that if we close the Catholic schools, where will we find time for any religious training or influence? This is a very real problem and does not even mention the time involved with after-school jobs or non-school entertainment such as movies and television. The Protestant Churches are faced with this problem, too, in operating Sunday schools.

Would it not be possible to include a department of religion in the curriculum of the public schools? Classes could be offered by all denominations and enrollment in these classes would be a matter of choice. Salaries of the teachers could be paid by the churches, and students who did not wish to enroll in a class in religion could take another elective. If all the churches would come together and support such a move, I do not think it would be too difficult to include courses in various religions in the public school system. In the United States there might be some questions of constitutionality that would have to be worked out first. But in other countries this is a possibility.

Another possibility would be for churches of several denominations to construct and maintain a religious education center very close to the public schools and conduct religion classes during "released" time. This is practical only if the religious education center is in close proximity to the public school and would be more practical on a secondary school level than on an elementary level. Some experiments are proceeding along this line.

But a serious effort must be made by the Church to provide religious education at all levels and for all members. Even if an attempt is made to keep some of the Catholic schools (and I am not advocating the elimination of all Catholic schools), the Church must take steps to provide religious training for children attending public schools and many more qualified priests and sisters to work with students at secular universities and with adults in various parish and community programs.

In recent years a permanent change has been introduced in the system of education as a result of the mass media. We are still accustomed to think of education primarily in terms of formal training in schools, but more and more people are being influenced by television, movies, radio, magazines, records, and newspapers. All these media represent an increase in the techniques available for education.

These media offer new opportunities, too, for the transmission of religious values, but there are few people with specific training in these fields being sought to work creatively in the Church to develop these new possibilities. Our efforts have been unimaginatively directed toward televising the Mass, for example, or broadcasting a sermon. But the possibilities are there. And the effectiveness of these media for the transmission of values is recognized. A televised drama, well-written and well-acted, dealing with the issue of racial segregation, for example, could help focus attention on the real moral dimensions of this problem, too often obscured by the "political" aspects. The utilization of audio-visual means at the Montreal Expo 67 gave a concrete expression of the existing possibilities.

We are in a world where the whole system of socialization in the Church is put in question. The Church must realize that the transmission of religious values is a collegial one and that it will not be accomplished just in the parish through the Sunday sermon or through the Catholic school system. As is true of society as a whole, the socialization process in the Church, which can be defined as the internalization of Christian values and the sense of belonging, has become a permanent process. We must constantly reinternalize the values and redefine our belonging in a changing society and in a changing Church. And this is not easy. But the people of God may expect this service from the institutional Church.

Many ways exist today, but we have not given enough attention to them. The Council showed the increased importance of mass communication. New expressions of the socialization process will develop, too, with the new understanding gained from the redefinition of the Church: the small community of worship (not being exclusive), the dialogued homily, new types of religious communities, and so on. The hope is that not too many obstacles will be placed in the way of their development.

THE COMMUNICATION SYSTEM

We have spoken about certain mechanisms in social institutions that are necessary for the functioning of the institution: norms, authority, and socialization. There remains the mechanism of *communication*.

Communication is one of the most important functions in any institution, and the manner in which it is organized and exercised is related directly to the interpretation of the aims of the institution. The effectiveness of the institution in achieving its aims will depend greatly upon how well the system of communication is serving its purpose. In the Church the function of communication is no less important. And in the post-conciliar Church this function is more important than ever if the aims of the Council are to be translated into action.

There are two main types of communication in an institution: *internal* and *external*.

Internal Communication

Communication *within* an institution becomes more complex as the institution itself grows in complexity. More crises come about because of difficulties in internal communication than because of any other factor. Actually, our knowledge of the organization of communication is rather primitive, and we are becoming more aware of this as we try to establish some systems of communication in the Church.

In a study of what communication is and of how it takes place, it becomes apparent that there are different types of internal communication.

The first type of communication, and the one with which we are most familiar in the Church, is a *one-way communication,* from the top to the bottom, from above to below: encyclicals, papal decrees and directives, pastoral letters from the bishop, and so on. These have too often been expressions of the concept of authority as it was understood before the Council, and many were characterized by their lack of concern for dialogue. Anyway, this was almost the only existing type of internal communication in the Church.

As it has been used, this type presented several difficulties. In the first place it has become psychologically unacceptable to modern man. An educated mind wants to know *why,* not only *what.* It wishes to engage in dialogue. And this is the great weakness of the one-way type of communication: there is no feedback.

Another difficulty is that often there is no communication, either, because very little care is given to the manner in which, for example, a pastoral letter is written, what language is used, whether the meaning is clear or completely obscured by "ecclesiastical doubletalk." There is no way of knowing whether the message has reached those whom it was intended to reach or whether it has been understood or accepted.

Since the Council, as ways are being sought to implement the new dimensions of the definition of the Church as the People of God, the need for a *two-way type of communication* is recognized. This means there must be some channels of communication set up which will allow information and ideas to travel from the periphery to the center. We have already discussed some of the structures that have been considered and in some places established for this: presbyterial councils, parish councils, pastoral councils, episcopal conferences, the Synod of bishops, and so on.

For these structures to function as they are intended, those in authority who are not very much used to listening to the opinions of others will have to accustom themselves to a new relationship with their people. This "collegial" relationship, based upon a recognition of each Christian's role as a responsible member of the Church, will bear little resemblance to the paternalistic approach

that characterized so many of the pre-conciliar relationships between hierarchy and people, or between the
"higher" clergy and the "lower."

A third type of internal communication is the development of a *public opinion* within the Church. This is
accomplished primarily through the use of the mass
media: magazines, newspapers, books, radio, television.
It is a very important type of communication in the
Church, but its importance is not necessarily recognized
by everyone. It had a very great effect, however, upon
the handling of the news releases of the Council, and it
is interesting to note what happened in order to understand the importance of the changes it occasioned.

At the beginning of the Council the *secret* was very
important, and even the sessions of the general assembly
could not be reviewed. Simultaneous translation was
suppressed because it was feared that persons outside
the walls would be able to hear what was going on inside
with the proper type of receiver. During the first session
of the Council the secret was something almost sacred,
and the only real information was coming through indis-
cretion.

There were press reports—of a sort—but they just
gave the names of the bishops who spoke and a short
account of what was said, never who said it. The journal-
ists had a hard time, but a secret cannot be kept by
nearly three thousand people even if they are bishops.
And soon the letters by "Xavier Rynne" were appearing

in the *New Yorker*, and Rome's morning newspaper, *Il Messagero*, was giving accurate accounts of the previous day's events, and all kinds of articles, books, and discussions were analyzing what was happening at the Council and why. A great effort was made to keep secret the fact that there were disagreements among the Council Fathers, but after all the press reports, it was no longer a secret.

By the time of the second session a much fuller report was given by the official Council press. At the third and fourth sessions the official organization of information was good.

The release of the information performed a liberating function in the Church. But in order to change the situation, the law of the secret had to be broken. And this brought a complete change in the Council.

The document on social communications is not one of the best of the Council, but since then there has been a growing awareness of the importance of information and communication in the life of the Church. The statement by the U.S. Bishops' Committee on Social Communications which asserts that man's right to be informed "is not a privilege conferred by an authority" but an inherent right "given him by God Himself" is an unequivocal acknowledgment of their belief in the right to information and the necessity of public opinion within the Church.

The last form of internal communication in the Church

could be called *horizontal communication,* and this is
needed especially among pastoral institutions because of
increased specialization in pastoral work.

Channels of horizontal communication are needed because of the necessity for collective pastoral action in
many areas, especially in larger cities but also in rural
areas. Communication will be greatly facilitated when a
council of priests is functioning in each diocese. In addition to the personal contact involved, minutes of each
meeting can be sent to every priest in the diocese following each meeting, and in this way they can all be
kept up-to-date on the questions that are before the
presbyterium and on the progress of the discussions.
Priests should be encouraged to submit suggestions and
observations to their "senators" to ensure that the de-
liberations of the priests' council will be representative
of the ideas and concerns of all the priests in the
diocese.

A further contribution to horizontal communication at this level of the Church could be an exchange
of ideas and information among the various diocesan
senates of priests. This would require some kind of central commission or secretariat to publish a newsletter,
and since many questions and problems are of concern
to priests across the nation, the experience and solutions
of one group could be instructive to others.

And the same is true for the pastoral councils where
lay people are represented. There, too, some channels of

horizontal communication will have to be organized in order to link together the local community, the diocesan pastoral council, some national bodies, and the international representation of laymen in the Church. It should not necessarily mean a big organization with a formal bureaucracy, but in a Church much less institutionalized in subsidiary activities, it will signify a real responsibility of Christians at all levels for what the Church has to be in the world.

External Communication

The second main type of communication in the Church exists with reference to the world outside the institution and may be called *external communication.*

This type of communication must also become a two-way process. In the past the emphasis has been placed on only one aspect: how does the Church present herself in the world and to the world? All the missionary work of the Church is external communication in the world. All the Church agencies in the public areas are in a type of communication with the world. But are we *in* communication with the world? And with what world? We may think that we are present in the world because we have churches and parishes all over, but what is the reality of this communication?

I already spoke of our general lack of competency in the mass media and the lack of utilization of the mass media as a whole. But there is not only a question of the *means* of communication. The external communication of the Church in the modern world is also, and perhaps principally, in the image the Church is conveying—not a fabricated image, but the real image the Church is presenting to the world.

Some signs are so important. Saying, for example, that we are the Church of the poor. How can we see that? What are we actually doing for and with the poor? That is the communication. All the accents of the Church, especially those things which are more visible in the Church, convey an image to the world. And what is most visible in the Church? The hierarchy, the priests, all those who are wearing the signs of the Church, who are visible almost all the time.

What is the communication to the world that was given by the grand pageant from the Renaissance that accompanies the installation of the "princes" of the Church, the cardinals? What do princes have to do with poverty? Or with the twentieth century? Were those really sacrilegious hands that wrote "Blessed are the poor" on the walls of a newly-purchased *nunciature* in Latin America? And do $200,000 convents built for a dozen nuns really convey the image of a "spirit of poverty"?

The secrecy, for example, which has surrounded the finances of the Vatican left room for all kinds of speculations. And these rumors, whatever the truth of the matter, will not be dispelled until the day when the Vatican, like the World Council of Churches, publishes its accounts and annual budgets.

We must be able, then, to look objectively at the image the Church is presenting to the world. It may be that the world is not rejecting Christ, but that it cannot see him mirrored through the clouded glass we are holding up to its view. And this is not related to our intentions; these may be excellent, and the message transmitted still negative.

All communication requires three things: a transmitter, a receptor, and a sign under the form of word (written or spoken) or symbol. In order to establish communication between those giving it and those receiving it, a certain common cultural zone must exist; otherwise the message will not be understood, because it must first be codified in signs and then de-codified. And this is very difficult in a pluralistic society where cultures tend no longer to exist in distinctly separate geographical areas, but are spread throughout the same given territory, and where this same territory is now becoming the whole world. This is why the Church must continue to find new ways and symbols to express the message of the Gospel which she is to communicate to all peoples.

The Church communicates in three ways: by *speaking* (and most of the time we have thought this was the only way), by *doing*, and by *being*. And there can be tremendous disparities between these three levels.

So the Church must be concerned with the type of external communication she gives to the world. But the communication of the Church with the world has to become a two-way process. We need a feedback for good communication. What does the world have to tell the Church? We have neglected this.

Reading the signs of the times, signs that God is giving us, is of great theological importance for the mission of the Church. We had ceased to receive this information from the world, and had even been trained to consider it insignificant. Our attitude too often has been that we had to give the truth to the world and that we did not have to accept any truth from the world.

But the Constitution of the Church in the Modern World emphasized that it is a duty of the Church, collectively speaking, to attend to the "signs of the times." It is not enough just to read newspapers or listen to television in order to get this information from the world. If the Church is to speak prophetically to the needs of the world, she must know these needs. How well are we really informed about the situation of mankind? We can have a renewed liturgy, and a restructured parish, and a reorganized seminary, but if the Church confines her concern to these internal reforms and does not direct her leadership to the real problems facing the world today, she will not communicate the sign of Christ's presence to the world or contribute to unity among men.

4 CRITICAL DECISIONS AND INSTITUTIONAL CHANGES

At one time or another every society experiences changes in its institutions, in roles, in patterns of behavior, in its individal members, and in its whole culture, its whole set of values. This type of change is called *social change*. It is a sign of life. However, when decisions affecting the definition of an institution itself and of its aims are arrived at, they may, as we have already noted, be termed "critical" because they provoke a rapid social change of all aspects of the institution. So there are some periods when social change is accelerated, and at these times the tensions and difficulties that normally accompany any change are greater. At present, as we have been stressing in this book, the Church is passing through a period of rapid social change not only in the secular world, as a result of technology, but within itself as an institution, as a result of the Council and its logical consequences.

In the consideration of social change in the Church

we will discuss three points: the *effects,* the *extension,* and the *rhythm* of social change.

THE EFFECTS OF CHANGE IN THE CHURCH

In a process of social change, and especially during a time of rapid social change, there will always be accentuated tensions between the *aims* of a social institution and the *organization.* This is, I think, very easy to understand.

A new definition in the aims, or a re-interpretation and change of emphasis, will automatically call into question all the ways previously used to accomplish these aims. The old ways of doing things may not be easily adapted to the new interpretation. This means that they will have to be changed, or abandoned completely, and new ways will have to be developed to accomplish the redefined aims.

The necessity for doing this, of course, has consequences on the whole organization, on all the roles and on all the secondary institutions connected with it. From the social point of view this involves a necessity to reorganize: to reorganize the work, but also to reorganize the structures, and to retrain the persons involved in these structures with a view to producing the mentality adapted to the new definition and the new orientation to action.

Of course the changes we are facing today are much more than just changes in organization. There is also a profound transformation in our vision of the world and in our understanding of revelation. It is true that there is a continuity in the Church, but continuity does not mean an identity of formulation or even an identity of belief. And I would make here a distinction between specific *beliefs* and the *faith* itself.

Our beliefs are closely related to the conception we have of the universe. This is quite apparent in the world view of the Bible or in the medieval spiritual expression of the faith. The belief in a heaven "above" us and a hell "below," for example, does not relate to our present knowledge of the cosmos. And many other things may have to come under the critical scrutiny of man progressing in the understanding of his universe.

But of course it is difficult to effect the necessary readjustment when we have been accustomed to regarding almost every belief as "sacred," with a strong Holy Office for the preservation of the "faith," and a rigid organization in the Church. The result is that some will not be able to distinguish sufficiently between the real content of the faith and the outmoded belief and will in fact, if not formally, abandon the faith. But another result is that a great number of the faithful of this generation will be profoundly troubled by the transformations in our vision of the world and in our understanding of revelation. The main temptation for the leaders of the Church may be to react along the old lines and in the old way in order to quiet these "doubts," and by refusing to recognize and assist in the real search in our time for faith, they may lose many in the present generation.

All this is provoking quite normally a tension between the actual organization and the perception of renewed aims in a period of rapid social change. It is much easier to see where changes should be made than it is to actualize these changes.

It is a sociological fact that every institution tends to be conservative. Because once behavior becomes a pattern, once this is formalized in roles, once these roles are organized around a function in an institution, which requires a social control, an elaboration of norms, the constitution of some form of authority—all this tends to combine in making change more complicated.

This is the paradoxical situation in which man lives as a social being: always under the necessity of institutional patterns of behavior, roles, institutions—or, in other words, always under the necessity of institutionalizing his social life—and at the same time always under the necessity of changing it.

It is the kind of apparent contradiction present all the time in society, but is it not a very rich reality? Through this dialectical process between the institutionalization and the change, society is progressing. On the one hand the institution tends to "fix" everything—patterns of action, of behavior, of belief—and fights against change. And on the other, in order to progress—and man tends to progress because he has a mind, because he is fundamentally active, because he wants to utilize nature, and because he received that dynamic energy from his Creator —man is always obliged to struggle against the paralyzing aspects of the institution.

This fundamental dialectical process is found in any society, in any social organization, and so also in the Church. As we have repeatedly emphasized, she is progressing through history by the will of God and under the guidance of the Holy Spirit, but through the ways and channels normal to men living together collectively. So the Church, too, will constantly experience this tension between institution and change.

From a psychological point of view, attitudes will always be of various types. Some people will be more prone psychologically to emphasize the institutional aspect of the Church, because it seems "safer." In a certain sense the whole traditional formation of priests and of Christians in general has tended to follow this line. In order to preserve the fundamental values of salvation, it seemed better to "conserve" what the Church had and not permit any experimentation or change for fear of the risk. This is the kind of mentality that will tend to avoid change and will go very far in fighting against change in the Church. Many of the difficulties, then, can be traced to a problem of basic personality, closely linked with certain attitudes toward the institution—any institution. At the other extreme we find progressives who are always seeking to destroy any type of institution, the anarchists or the "perpetual revolutionaries." For them the revolution is an aim in itself and not a means, and as soon as one revolution is over they are already thinking ahead to the next.

The *continuum* between the conservative-integralist and the revolutionary mentality is a very interesting psychological problem. A study of these basic types would probably reveal many similarities. We would also find these same basic mental attitudes operating in other Christian churches and among the Communist party factions. This is not to say that everything is just a matter of psychological determinism. There is much more to it than that. But these attitudes must be expected in the Church because she is made up of men.

To summarize: human reactions to society come from the nature of social life itself as well as from individual personality tendencies. These normal reactions are accentuated in a period of rapid social change, and the tensions between the aims of the institution and its organization and between conservative and progressive personalities as well are heightened.

When the tension becomes so great that the institution cannot absorb the changes into its structures, a real conflict arises. As pressure for change is building up in an institution, the conflict generally arises in a group when a few people manifest some dissatisfaction in a collective way. This can be through writing, through teaching, through group protest, but the conflict occurs when the first manifestation of dissatisfaction is demonstrated socially.

Then we have all kinds of processes where the relationship between the protesting group or individual and the institution is adjusted—for better or worse. There can be a very strong retaliation from the institution where the action taken is intended to destroy the dissenting group or individual through expulsion. This can happen in the Church, for example, through excommunication, through censorship, or through creating such circumstances that the protestor just quits the institution.

Or the institution can also attempt to neutralize a dissenter or a protest group in another way, through giving some kind of recognition and trying to move the leaders of the protest movement inside the institution to some post of responsibility where they will have to care more about the institution than about the new trends. This way has sometimes been used in the Church when a priest was made a monsignor with the expectation that he would then keep quiet. It does not always work. And of course not all our monsignors were incipient protestors!

When a group does leave an institution it is usually a progressive group, convinced that there is no way of changing the institution from within. It sometimes happens that a conservative group will leave, such as the Old Catholics after Vatican I, but this is rare because it is so contrary to their position. What usually happens is that they establish a schism in fact, without leaving the institution. This is what is happening today in some places.

In France, for example, some conservative groups have been fighting vigorously against the Council and against the changes in the Church. At the same time they claim to be faithful to the Pope and even to the Council. Conservative writers, such as Michel de Saint Pierre, are having an influence in Europe, particularly in the conservative milieu. Such writings are doing harm in the Church and are influencing people who are not integralists themselves but are dissatisfied with the changes in the Church because they don't understand them. Some of these writers go so far as to say: "You see what is happening in the Church? You are dissatisfied? Well, it is much more serious than you think! It is a whole plot to ruin the Church, and this is a diabolical enterprise organized by the Masons, the Jews, the Communists." Of course, those are extreme cases.

But an institution may also integrate changes. This is perhaps one of the most important testimonies given in a changing world by the Catholic Church in the Council: that she was able to accept changes, and very important ones, not only in a reshaping of the façade, but in a revision of values. The problem of the post-conciliar Church is to take care that the word "aggiornamento" does not become a symbol applied only to outward appearances, with no corresponding application to a renewal in values. A computer in a chancery is not neccesarily the best sign of reform and renewal!

So the effect of social change on an institution is to accentuate the tension between the aims of the institution and its organization. And an organization can react to the resulting tensions in one of two ways: by refusing them and trying to oust or neutralize the dissenters in one way or another *or* by accepting tension as a part of growth and trying to find ways to experiment and to institutionalize needed change without provoking needless conflict.

THE EXTENSION OF CHANGE

We have examined the various elements of an institution and some of the ways in which an institution is functioning: norms, authority, socialization, communication. A social change may occur in one element or another. There may be a change, for example, in some process of socialization or in some pattern of authority, or in some roles. When there are changes in many elements occurring at the same time, the social change is quite profound, because all these elements are interrelated. When there is a change in one role this will change other roles. When one institution is changed, the others are affected, too. All this is happening today in the Church.

In the last five or six years almost every element of the institutional Church has been put in question directly by the Council or indirectly because of the accent put on the definition of the Church as the people of God.

For example, the definition of the Church as the people of God, further extended by the concept of the presence of the Church in the world, results in a totally new approach to the action of the Christian in the world and to the expression of the Christian community. Now we are becoming more and more aware of the fact that it is in the Christian's commitment in the world that he will encounter God and contribute to the unity of mankind. Therefore the old concept of Catholic Action as part of the hierarchical mission in the Church is already dead. This is why, I think, we see conflicts between the hierarchy and the lay leaders of Catholic Action movements in different parts of the world. The lay leaders want to be involved in a concrete, visible, and collective commitment in political, social, and economic problems. They do not see how they, as Christians, can do less. The hierarchy, on the other hand, does not admit that the Church as institution should be committed to specific objectives in secular society. Both are right. It is the problem which is wrongly raised, because Catholic Action as we have known it in the past, directed and defined by the hierarchy, can no longer substitute for the responsibility of all Christians for the mission of the Church in the world. It has been a useful and even a necessary step in the Church, but its day is over. In short, we can now recognize that the responsibility for the mission of the Church in the world today belongs to every member of the people of God, and is not the responsibility only of the institutional Church. Christians will continue to come together in various forms of groups, but no longer with the orientation implied by "Catholic Action." They will define for themselves their own goals: religious formation, spirituality, charitable action, action in society, and so on. And with the exception of prayer and worship, they will assemble to accomplish these objectives not just with other Catholics or even only with other Christians, but with all men who share similar goals.

But the definition of the Church as the people of God is such that it will "percolate" to all aspects of the Church's existence. And if we take this concept seriously, it will also extend, for another example, to our concepts of religious art and architecture.

In the World Congress of Religion, Architecture, and Visual Art held in New York in 1967, a great deal of discussion was centered on these concepts. It was agreed that religious architecture reflected the values of the Christian community, and was especially a reflection of the way the Church conceived of her presence in the world. For example, to see the church as a dominating building in the neighborhood or in the city images the conception of a certain "domination" of society by the religious institution. The image of the Church as servant in the world, however, will bring us to a new conception of what the church building has to be.

Our renewed perception of the world as the place where God lives and acts and where the Christian lives and acts also gives opportunity for the expression in all architecture of some spiritual reference. In a certain paradoxical way the full acceptance of a secularized world can give all architecture a religious significance when it expresses, says Edward Sovik, "the conviction that the universe and its parts are held together; that there is an order which can supply meaning to our lives and all that surrounds them; that there is a design which wraps past, present and future in one package, which makes sense of both inert and lively, motion and rest, space and solid, reason and feeling."

Church architecture must be related to the work of Christians in the world. The church building is not a symbol of power or of pride. It is the meeting place where the Christian community expresses liturgically and sacramentally the profound meaning of its existence: the union with God and the unity with all mankind.

But if we really conceive the Church as servant, we will have to revise the use made of our churches. Why should such a building serve only on Sundays? Could it be at the disposal of the whole community? How? And what will this mean for church architecture? After all, in the Christian vision of the world there are no "sacred places," but only places where man works out his sanctification. For a long time we have separated the world from the place of sanctification. Now we see that there is no separation: the world is the place where the Christian sanctifies himself, and this may not be separated from the necessary expression and source of union with God and unity with man. Everywhere Christians meet for this "actualization" of the Eucharistic community, there is a holy event, and this may be in the living room of a family, the Yankee Stadium or the parish church.

Yet churches will be necessary, otherwise Christianity would be completely dissolved in the world, which may be the ideal of the Kingdom, but would not be very realistic on earth if we know very much about the concrete existence of human beings. But our conception of these churches will be different; they will be expressions of the Christian community as a sacrament in the world. In this regard, we will have also to abandon the idea of building cathedrals as signs of prestige. The church of the bishop is a symbol, important today also, but not the symbol of the power of the prince. The great assemblies of Christians which take place on special occasions may be very well and even better organized in the normal meeting places of the community: stadia, squares, centers, halls, and so on. Modern expressions of art and other media of visual art can help adapt to each occasion the symbolic environment where such gatherings happen.

These are only two examples of the extension of change. It goes further than we thought, perhaps, but this is the living Church.

THE RHYTHM OF CHANGE

In addition to the extension of social change, or the number of changes, there is another aspect to social change: the *rhythm* or timing of the changes.

It is readily understood that if the process of change is extended over a long period of time, it will be easily accepted and absorbed by the institution, although the first actual change that is introduced may still create somewhat of a shock. But over a period of time the institution will be able to adapt, to change a structure, and the lag between the organization and the developing values will not be too great.

However, when there is a very sudden change—for example, in the definition of a role—the possibilities of tension are greatly increased because all those exercising this role will have to adapt themselves to this new definition. This will be very difficult for many to do. In these days of rapid communication a great many people will be aware of the new definitions and their expectations of a transformation in the role will be increased. Thus the anticipation of change may outstrip the institutionalization of change, and this time lag can easily lead to the frustration and disappointed hopes.

This is true for all the institutional aspects of the Church and, as a matter of fact, we are facing a very rapid change, one that is not only global, in the sense that it is affecting nearly all the institutions and roles in the Church, but is also very sudden.

This is due mostly to the fact that the Church had been envisioned mainly as a *non-changing institution.* Just a few years ago when we were studying ecclesiology one of the main qualities which was attributed to the Church was that she was non-changing, that she was always the same. And of course in the most fundamental sense this is true. The Church is always the same. But the Church will always be the same in a changing world if she is able to change, and this was forgotten. Transcendence had been identified with immobility and faithfulness with paralysis!

The vision of the Church as a non-changing institution brought with it the absolutization of all kinds of relative aspects of the life of the Church, in the structure, in the roles, and also in the norms. So much so that many Catholics were actually identifying themselves according to these aspects: the Latin in the liturgy, the Eucharistic fast, Friday abstinence, novenas, the rosary, the nine "First Fridays," special costumes for religious, and so on.

So many of these relative aspects of the institutional Church were treated as so essential to the life of Christians that the day the Church began to change many of them, or to de-emphasize some of them, it brought a real shock to many people, and among them many priests. Their image of the Church was of such a stable institution that any change would have created a shock, but so many changes coming in such a short period created a situation that was almost traumatic for some people. We must understand this and try to meet the situation pastorally, but without being hampered in our efforts at renewal in the Church.

But what was a shock for some was a great deliverance for others who had been hoping for these changes for a long time. In fact in a great part of the Church a consciousness grew very rapidly that most of the changes should have been made long ago and that many of the former rules and practices had created more of a barrier than a vehicle between the people and the message of Christ.

The changes also proved positive outside the Catholic Church, because as long as she appeared to the world as an institution unable to adapt or to change, the Church was not really relevant to a changing world and held no meaning or message for it. But by seeing the need for change, by being able to change without negating any of the essential aims of her mission, the Church will henceforth be able to speak to the modern world in a more meaningful way.

As we have repeatedly emphasized, in the post-conciliar Church we must expect tensions, conflicts, and even crises. The tensions may be important or not, quite serious or not, leading to conflicts or not. But the tensions themselves are creative and a very positive factor in modern society. They are either a sign of change or an indication of an awareness of the necessity for change. As long as they remain tensions they manifest that a change is already happening in one way or another. It is only when tensions lead to conflict or to a crisis that we have a situation that is not normal or desirable.

But we have been so used to evaluating positively a situation of "no change," that as soon as we hear about tensions in the Church we react negatively or try to deny their existence, as happened at the beginning of the Council. It was as if tensions in the Church threatened her very existence. This is because tensions had been thought of only in a negative way.

But tensions in any kind of institution, including the Church, are a good sign, a sign of life and a means of progress. A society in which everyone is convinced that the ultimate goal has finally been reached, where no further progress seems necessary or possible, is in danger of dying. And we have seen that happen in history.

However, tensions can lead to conflicts and crises. And

of course by now it should be obvious that we regard tensions as normal and creative and crises as negative and destructive in an institution. A crisis is an open conflict which should not have had to happen.

When will tensions lead to conflicts or to crises? There are two ways. The first is when the authority in an institution, stressing the importance of the institutional aspects and emphasizing always the risk and the danger of change, strongly resists needed change. The stronger the resistance the greater will be the crisis. The force of authority will then be employed to try to break the movement towards change.

But there is also another way for tensions to lead to crises. And this is when the people who are pressing for change—in the liturgy, in the role of the priest, in pastoral work, in catechetics—have a weak theological background. When the desire for change is not built on a deep theological vision of the Church, the reason given for the change is apt to become just an ideology, a slogan.

Before the Council, for example, there were some attempts to adapt the liturgy to modern culture, and of course those making them had the great merit of trying, and of seeing the necessity of doing this, but many were not very well grounded in a real knowledge of the liturgy, its history, and its theological function in the Church. And the results were not very satisfactory. It is only since the study of the liturgy, its history and theology included, has begun that a real transformation and reform has been possible. This transformation is still going on and is now almost ready to make major steps.

Experiments in the pastoral field should not be avoided because they will not always be successful. We must expect to make some mistakes. There would be no need to experiment if we were sure of success. And in fact, in a Church which takes renewal seriously there will be a continuing need for experimental activity. Experiments should not be undertaken only "just to see what happens," but should have a reasonable basis and offer some hope of success. They should have some well-defined aims and, if possible, be conducted without too much publicity.

In summary: changes which are not based on sound theology will provoke crises and conflict, as will the adamant resistance to change on the part of the authority in an institution. Social change is an important factor in the life of all institutions. It is productive of tensions which if rightly channeled can give a creative impetus leading to needed change and renewal and if repressed and ignored can erupt into open crises and destructive conflicts.

5 HOPES AND CRISES

So many ideas and situations are evolving in the Church today that it would be unwise to come to any premature conclusions. We can expect, however, that the transformation of authority and communication in the institutional Church will reflect the different reactions which have characterized the response of some members of the hierarchy and some lay people to the changes brought by the Council.

Some see the Council as a catastrophe for the Church and view their role in the post-conciliar Church as one of salvage. They will try to save what can be saved and will use authority to resist change as though it were an occasion of sin.

Others are the progressives of yesterday who are the conservatives of today. They think the Council went far enough and that nothing more needs to be done.

It is even possible that many who regard themselves as

most progressive are still so conditioned by the old absolutist-triumphalist mentality that without being really aware of it they expected an almost immediate absolute reform and renewal, so that the Church would have triumphed again, although in another way. Many have accepted the idea of a pilgrim Church but are embarrassed by the reality. Some who sought change are much less prepared to live with the ferment of change.

And there are others who see the necessity for institutionalizing change, for making it possible for the Church to function in a permanent state of reflection and with established mechanisms for change and adaptation.

Long-awaited changes in the Curia have now been effected in an almost unexpected way. It is too soon to make predictions about the manner in which the reform will be applied, but the changes brought about in the structures are oriented in the direction indicated by the Council and in line with the exigencies of the modern world.

In some areas laymen have formed their own associations, unconnected with the hierarchy, to speak their minds about renewal in the Church. This is a new phenomenon and it will be instructive to observe its development and influence. And in many dioceses, pastoral and presbyterial councils are functioning, and already some interdiocesan communication is taking place.

But many of the developments of the post-conciliar Church receive little publicity and some may never be recorded. It may not be possible to record the most significant changes because these have to do with the internalization of the spirit of the Council in the lives of the people of God.

However, the conservative reaction is still very powerful. The frequent appeals for obedience and faith appear to be directed more to faith and obedience to the previous structures than to the Church of the living Christ. And the continued warnings and repeatedly expressed fears of modern thought could dissipate the advances into the modern world made by the Council. One cannot accept the signs of the times as coming from God and at the same time reject them as the work of the devil. The Council may have accepted the modern world, but it is clear that too many in the Church still have not, even if the ambiguity of all human enterprise is recognized and the presence of sin seen as the dramatic situation of mankind.

We shall be better able to make an adjustment to the tension accompanying the evolution of change in the structures of the post-conciliar Church if we see it as a sign of life, as normal. Impatience with the rate of change may be more bearable if we remind ourselves of the number of needed changes which have actually been accomplished in just a few years.

But we must be able to accept the uncertainties and frustrations as well as the enormous possibilities of living as adult Christians in a changing Church in a changing world. We must forego the illusion of final solutions and learn to live with dynamic equilibrium in an incarnate Church where, as in every institution, the recognition of needed change will always outrun the implementation of that change.

The gap between the recognition and the implementation will be considerably lessened, however, if the conciliar values of participation, collegiality, personal responsibility, and freedom become the spirit of all the structural reforms in the Church. These are the values of maturity, and the task of all in the post-conciliar Church if we are to grow up in Christ, to come of age as the people of God. And there are two main areas which will be crucial: *the relations between Church and world* and *the emerging Christian communities.*

THE CHURCH IN THE WORLD

It is at precisely this point—the relations between the Church and the world—that the fundamental hope and the test of the success or failure of the Council lies. If we lose our concern for the problems of the world, the Council will have failed. The Church will be meaningless for the world. In an age of relative tolerance the world will not persecute the Church, but will just turn aside.

Pope Paul's encyclical, *Populorum Progressio,* has taken a very positive approach to some of the world problems.

At the *Pacem in Terris* Convocation held in Geneva in 1967, references to Pope Paul's encyclical were as numerous as those to Pope John's. It was an extraordinary experience to see how seriously people of all beliefs were discussing what the Popes had to say about the common problems of mankind. The world expects the Church to speak on these problems, to speak to the conscience of man. And when she does not speak, she is held culpable.

What will characterize the relations between the Church and the world? First, we will need a real understanding of the world in which we are living and second, a real concern for the whole drama of mankind. We must be involved as Church, community and institution, in the problems of peace, of race relations, of the cybernetic revolution, of development, of population, of culture. These must be the concerns of the Church because these are the concerns of humanity which has been saved by Christ.

During the preparation of *Gaudium et Spes* we saw how far we were from a real theology of creation and of the "new" creation. We still lack adequate theological thinking to meet the present problems of development, population, culture, peace, cybernetics.

We need, according to the words of Joseph Sittler, the Protestant theologian of Chicago University, a "new discourse" to meet the new situation of man in the world today. Without doubt this is one of the most important tasks for the Church. The work of the theologians in rethinking religious values, expressions, and symbols is essential.

This is a permanent task. A great deal of modern atheism is the result of a false or incomplete presentation of the faith. *Gaudium et Spes* affirms that in many cases atheism is more an affirmation of man than a negation of God. Leslie Dewart, in his book *The Future of Belief,* urges the necessity of a reformulation of belief, even of a new concept of God. The same concern is expressed in a certain way by Bonhoeffer in his refusal of the "religious" or by the theologians of "the death of God."

In a time of research we must not be too much afraid of the efforts at new formulations. Of course erroneous ones may be proposed, but we have to recognize that we are permanently in a situation of research and that no formulation can be the last word here below. And this takes nothing away from the absolute certitude of the faith. We are in an age of doctrinal humility, where the danger of dissolution will not be met by intransigence but by humble recognition that we believe in a "hidden God," that "now we are seeing a dim reflection in a mirror" with the firm hope of seeing him face to face when the Kingdom will be achieved with the second coming of Christ and the "recapitulation" of the whole creation in him.

The Council did adopt a positive view of the world, which was a real change from the previous concept viewing progress as competition with God. It accepted the reality that man lives in a changing world and that in order to be faithful to the mission given by Christ, one of the first spiritual duties of the Church is to read "the signs of the times." It opened the way for new theological elaboration, already in great progress today.

All of this must be implemented now in our actions in the world as Christians. This can be a great ecumenical work because these are the tasks facing all the Christian churches. The establishment at the Vatican of a perma-nent commission for World Justice and Peace offers hope that the Church will sustain her commitment to the prob-lems of modern man. It also offers the possibility for co-ordinating and cooperating with representatives of other religious bodies, such as the World Council of Churches, in programs and policies for peace and development.

At the meeting of the World Conference on Church and Society sponsored by the World Conference of Churches at Geneva in 1966, the participants urged upon the churches an involvement in political, social and eco-nomic affairs as churches, to perform a prophetic role in society. And this was not just a conference of clerics. More than two-thirds of those participating were lay peo-ple.

If the Church is a sign, one of the first consequences is its *prophetic role* in the world. This will be realized ac-cording to a double dimension: the *edification of the future* and *judgment on society.*

The *edification of the future* is the eschatological aspect

of the prophetic function. This cannot be expressed only
by words, it must be expressed by deeds. What man
makes of this earth is not indifferent to the new creation.
But a constant reference to the world to come must be
made in order to see further than a mere belief in "progress" or in the "affluent society." J. B. Metz writes that
we are workers building this future, and not mere inter-
preters of this future. This prophetic role will help believers to take this world seriously.

The religious community has also the function of already actualizing this future here on earth. It will not be
accomplished by an identification with a given society or
culture. This would mean the secularization of religion.
The Church actualizes the union with God through
prayer, mystical life, sacrament. This is the sense of the
Eucharist in the Christian Church. But she actualizes
also the union of all mankind through love, universality,
unity. This is symbolized in the sacramental community,
the Eucharistic community.

The prophetic function is oriented toward this world
as well as the world to come and therefore a *judgment on
society* is also the task of the Church. She is not of this
world and her participation in society must always be
critical. She must put into question a world which takes
itself for its own goal. Therefore the struggle for justice,
for equality, for universal love will be a very important
function. It will be her role to denounce all injustice in
every society and also to indicate the meaning of the

evolution of the whole of mankind, not only of a privileged few. And this role is based not only on charity and mercy but on the vocation of all humanity to prepare the new creation.

The concrete performance of this task will consist, first of all, in giving *orientation* to society. To give meaning to the collective task of man requires different levels of orientation. The first one is what Paul Ricoeur calls "the necessary utopia," meaning by this the unity of mankind. Religious communities must reformulate this in each culture and for each time, in order to recall mankind to its aim. And although in a certain way this is a utopia, because we know that the unity of mankind will never be fully accomplished on earth, yet it is a necessary utopia and a real goal for the achievement of mankind because this is the way through which History will join the Kingdom.

But the general orientation to the unity of mankind is not enough. Man needs some precisions, some "middle-range axioms." The unity of mankind will be realized by *pacem in terris,* or by the realization of a "responsible society." And going even further, the Church must indicate some ways, not in the sense of giving all the answers, but of making the message concrete. An example of this is the encyclical of Paul VI, *Populorum Progressio.*

For the concrete orientation of the action of Christians and of all men in society, the insistence will be more on *values* than on norms. In a complex, specialized, and mobile society, norms are rapidly becoming inadequate. The accent will be put on values to orient the behavior in social life.

And finally, the importance of *prophetic gestures* as a way of giving orientation, of protesting against injustices, will be very significant. Peace today is the fundamental requisite for development, and the war in Vietnam has been the greatest obstacle. Land reform is the condition of economic and social take-off in developing countries. Equal opportunities in education, jobs, and housing are pre-requisites for the full participation of all races in a society. If the Church is not concerned with these problems, she will be irrelevant in modern society and, as a consequence, unable to be the sign she is supposed to be. One of the ways of expressing such a concern is the performance of prophetic gestures, recalling to societies their duties or indicating the way to be followed. This will be just as necessary in the future as it is today because in the society of the future revolutions will not happen without injustice any more than they do now: the cybernetic revolution tends to bring social injustices similar to those associated with the industrial revolution.

To respond to these problems of mankind, therefore, the religious community must be able to perform the indicated tasks in a continuous way, through all the channels and all the means of expression at its disposal. This is not possible in any society through some vague individual faith. It is only possible through what we, as

Christians, would call a *church,* which means an *institution* able to express itself at different levels in society.

And this is why, even though our first concern should not be for the ecclesiastical institution but for the people for whom the Church exists, there must be serious attention given to the reform and renewal of the institution because the institution is necessary in order to make the Church able to speak effectively to the needs of all mankind.

EMERGING FORMS OF THE CHRISTIAN COMMUNITY

The Church, being a sign, must be perceived as such by man. A response to the needs of man does not mean that the Church is to perform the social and psychological functions of society. She represents a general answer over and above all the concrete needs, not primarily an answer to the immediate and particular needs, but a reference to the transcendent which gives a *general meaning to life* and gives the certainty, not yet experienced, of a final answer (faith).

This answer includes of course the meaning of death, a step toward resurrection and a sign of the provisional aspect of this world. In a world longing for the resurrection, it gives a meaning to death, which is the refusal to consider the immediate as definitive, and also gives hope of what Teilhard called "this unique and supreme event, where History must join Transcendence." It includes also the sense of our personal and collective failures and the dramatic aspect of the history of humanity. The Kingdom and the new creation will not just happen, with no reference to our own achievement. In a way they will be also what we have made of this world through our efforts, and in this work the responsibility and the liberty of man are involved.

The Church gives such an answer to the needs of people by the transmission of the word of God and the whole process of socialization and also by worship, the expressive function of religion.

She not only gives man an answer to his own meaning and situation, but also furnishes a *sense of belonging* to a community, which already anticipates the Kingdom. This community will have various forms according to cultures and societies, but it will never be identified with the natural group, even if its concrete realization corresponds to this dimension. Otherwise the religious community will only add a ritual dimension to the group and will not be a reference to the Kingdom.

But in order to be an efficient sign, the Church must speak to man in his own language, in reference to his values, attitudes, and behavior, to his culture and to his situation in the world. The sign must be meaningful. And in the modern world the Church will encounter the present situation of man in an age of technological revolution.

In a pretechnical civilization the religious institution—
in most cases the parish—was in charge of many functions
and the priest was the social leader. But, as we have
stressed throughout this book, we are no longer living in
this type of civilization. Ours is a secularized, mobile,
urban society. And for the Church, the Christian community in a highly specialized and socialized society, this
will mean a role which will become less and less a "sup-
portive" one. She will no longer be in charge of the many
functions which were hers in a pretechnical civilization
but will have a much more specific part to play. In sociological language we would say that the Church is performing fewer and fewer instrumental functions in society and is tending to be confined to more expressive
functions. This does not mean—especially in view of what
we said earlier about the role of the Church in the world
—that religion is a mere ritualistic function, detached
from the mission of man in the world.

The Church has internal as well as external aims, and
her internal aims are directed toward forming *a community of believers.*

In order to carry out all her aims, therefore, the Church
must take some social form or forms. In other words, the
Church must be visible in society, she must be able to be
seen, to be recognized. This is a necessity in terms of her
members as well, if they are to be able to develop a sense
of identity with the religious community.

These social forms must be related to the situation of

man, that is, they must be in accord with the type of civilization in which he finds himself.

So in a society which is urban, mobile, and secularized, the following characteristics will be found in the emerging forms of the Christian community. It will be *pluridimensional,* composed of *monovalent institutions,* having *participation in leadership,* fulfilling *expressive functions with a symbolic dimension,* and at all times *institutionalizing change.*

Of these five characteristics, the first three concern the structural aspect of the Christian community, the fourth, the cultural aspect, and the fifth, both structural and cultural aspects.

Let us now examine a little more precisely what this means.

Pluridimensional Form

The internal aims of the religious institution refer to worship (the expressive function), to the internalization of values, attitudes, and behavior (socialization), and to the creation of a sense of belonging (cohesion of the group). To realize these aims in the present and in the future society, a *pluridimensional form* is necessary. In order to simplify we will distinguish only three levels: the small group, the congregation, and the large community; but some intermediary ones could be added. All three levels are necessary and no one of them may be substituted for any other.

The *small group* is characterized by the affective links which exist among its members. It supposes a face-to-face relationship. It has been said sometimes that in our society the small group, or "primary" group, was disappearing. But this is not true. What is true is that the basis of the formation of small groups has shifted from a local geographical or family dimension to a great variety of social, professional, and cultural affinities. Modern society makes possible many choices in determining the formation of small groups.

We also find a diversity of small groups formed for religious purposes, and it would be a mistake to try to limit them artificially only to a geographical base for worship. For many people the dimension of worship in the small group seems necessary. In the Catholic Church, the absence of some liturgical function at this level has occasioned considerable efforts to introduce some of the sociological characteristics of the small group at the congregational level, but with many failures. The small group, however, will be only one dimension of the Christian community, and it must resist the temptation to identify itself as the Eucharistic community. There must always be a wider dimension. In some Protestant denominations the sect-like small group, in being almost the only reference to a community, has the effect of reducing the perspectives to just the closed group. This is why worship at this level should not become a weekly, permanent objective.

The *congregation* is the first step toward greater universality. For many people it will be the only concrete experience of a certain universality. Therefore the congregational level must be open, not restricted to one social, ethnic, professional, or age group. It must be oriented toward the universal community of believers and, through it, to the universal community of man.

In modern society the congregation will be less and less determined by the geographical residence. In a mobile society, where choice is one of the very important values, the voluntary aspect of belonging to a given congregation will be accentuated. The members of the congregation (the parish) will be all believers participating in an activity, especially worship, on this level. And this is also true for the passing or touring faithful joining a worshipping congregation of people.

The level of the *large community* is the third social form of the Christian community. The planetarization of the world will only be met at this level. A prophetic function for the whole of mankind supposes a worldwide community. The dynamic modern man will not be satisfied by a community expressing itself only on a group or even on a congregational level. He will feel that such a religious community is meaningless for his broader aspirations and preoccupations. In a certain respect we may say that not only theoretically, but also sociologically, the two other local levels will make sense only in reference to a universal community.

The expressions of this community level will be various. The mass media have a great role to play, giving to each person the opportunity of identifying himself with the universal Church or the religious community through specific events; these will help to maintain a sense of belonging and to transmit religious values. The World Council of Churches is playing an important role in creating a sense of the union of the Christian churches. Its action has been especially valuable in the analysis of, and the positions taken toward, the great social problems of mankind today. But the expression of universality may also be created by great manifestations of religious devotion, or assemblies gathering people from all over the world. In a time of so many international congresses this type of expression is surely not out of date. And finally the expression of universality may exist in a person, as it does in the Roman Catholic Church in the person of a John XXIII or Pope Paul.

Monovalent Institutions

The religious community has also been affected by the specialization of modern society, and specialized institutions characterize the modern Church. In an earlier society, as we have said, only one religious institution, the parish or the local congregation, was needed for almost all the religious functions. Now specialized institutions are numerous: movements of spirituality, centers of information, pastoral services for catechesis, liturgy, and so on, groups for charitable work, publications, and the like. These services are not all organized around one polyvalent institution. They tend, on the contrary, to be performed by specialized institutions because they require more and more specialized skills. This results in a more and more specialized role for the priest as well.

It would be a mistake, in the society of the future, to make efforts to revive a polyvalent type of institution—and some of the present pastoral efforts seem bent in such a direction. On the contrary, we must favor a great variety of monovalent institutions. The level of coordination will be no longer the local level of the parish but some regional unit (the diocese, or for certain functions a division of the diocese like the deanery) or the national territory (Bishops' Conference or National Council of Churches) or even the continent (the CELAM: Latin American Bishops' Council).

Leadership and Participation

In the sociological situation of man today, participation of the members in the religious institution will be of great importance. Belonging is no longer automatically assured because one has been born in this family or in that village or region. Participation must be developed at all levels: small group, congregation, and large community and also for all functions: worship, communication, socialization.

This will necessitate a redefinition of the religious leadership in the Church. If specifically religious roles remain necessary, they will no longer be automatically accompanied by social prestige and social power. They will be more specialized to correspond to the real pastoral needs of the people. Religious leaders will be evaluated in terms of their performance more than by their consecration. The phenomenon of a "clerical cast" will be less accepted, and we will know many diversified forms of ministries, most probably not identified only with the full-time celibate priest.

Expressive Functions and Symbolism

When most of the natural bases for belonging to a religious community are disappearing (which means a purification of religion), the social and psychological content of the expressive function must be reinforced. It is the function of the Church to express, to show forth, to be the *sign* of close union with God and of the unity of all mankind, and this will happen especially through worship. But the worship of God takes place in a community of men and so attention must be given to the social and psychological aspects related to this action. We will have to develop different types of worship to be realized at the three levels of the Christian community that we examined before: the small group, the congregation, and the large community.

It seems that the first (small group) and the last (large community) do not need a specific space. The small group is close to realism and must meet in ordinary places with a minimum of ritualism. The large community has only occasional gatherings, and it will ordinarily use common places of meeting, like a stadium or a main square. Only exceptionally will a specific place be built, when the repetition of such gatherings justifies it, as is the case, for example, for places of pilgrimage.

On the other hand, as we have already pointed out, the congregational level does seem to require a specific place in order to fulfill its expressive function, a building. Such a building gives the opportunity to express in a symbolic way a reference to the transcendent. But if it gives a specific opportunity for symbolism, it is surely not an exclusive one. Everything that functions as a sign of the Church has a symbolic dimension.

Symbolism in modern society is becoming more important, and this will have an effect on the Church. Her expressive function will be realized by means that go beyond verbal communication. Of course this has always been so, but it is becoming even more so today. The development of audio-visual communication is related to this reality.

Symbolism has always been used in the liturgy and is very closely related to it. If on the level of the small group the symbolism must be very simple and close to reality, the renewal of symbolism at the level of the congregation is also very important. I do not think this will be a matter of adopting symbols drawn from the world of technology, however. An attempt to create technical symbols in the liturgy or for the sacraments most probably would not signify a reference to the transcendent because the technical world is the expression of the "artifact," of what has been made by man, and so of what is fully "secularized." But there is not only the problem of a renewal of symbolism but also the probability that a great many of our present symbols are actually in contradiction to the transcendent reality we try to signify. Only more empirical research and experiment can be helpful in this renewal.

Institutionalization of Change

We are living not only in a period of change, but in a civilization characterized by change. This is why in the Church and in all the religious communities of the Church we have to institutionalize change. This will involve an institutionalization of change both in the structural and in the cultural aspects of the Church. Otherwise she will be the witness and the conservatory of past civilization. This is the constant temptation of an institution whose function it is to indicate what is transcendent, what is not-changing. But even if it is a paradox, the only way to be the witness of the non-changing is to be able to express this witness in a living way in a changing society.

The emerging forms of Christian communities are not dreams of the future. They already exist. In many countries we are already witnessing the birth of specific groupings of Christians, manifesting a solid belief in the priestly, prophetic, and ministerial aspect of their baptism, signifying by their service of humanity the active presence of Christ in the world. The liturgical experiments are attempts to discover the various types of expression for these Christian communities. And in some areas the government of the Church is becoming more democratized.

But the weight of the past is heavy, and there is reason for some to complain about their "outmoded" Church. To find new ways in a period of such rapid transformations is not easy, however; there must be patient experimentation and time for reformulations on the institutional level. This cannot be carried out only in the quiet of the theologian's cell or in the shelter of well-defined experimental groups. Experiments cannot be carried out in abstraction, entirely detached from the life of the concrete community. We are living in a world of communication where "the medium is the message," and where the theologian must be confronted with the live currents of ideas.

So the wake of Vatican II will bring tensions, crises, conflicts, and hopes to the mainstream of the Church. But there is no need to be afraid of this, for these are all aspects of the same great reality: life. And for the Christian—and for the Church—there can be no greater promise.

INDEX

189

ate Due